Learn AutoCAD® LT for Windows™ in a Day

Ralph Grabowski

Wordware Publishing, Inc.

Library of Congress Cataloging-in-Publication Data

Grabowski, Ralph.
    Learn AutoCAD LT for Windows in a day / Ralph Grabowski.
      p. cm.
    Includes index.
    ISBN 1-55622-426-5
    1. Computer graphics.   2. AutoCAD LT for Windows.   I. Title.
    T385.G69253   1994
    604.2'0285'5369--dc20
                                                            94-16806
                                                                  CIP

Copyright © 1995, Wordware Publishing, Inc.

All Rights Reserved

1506 Capital Avenue
Plano, Texas 75074

No part of this book may be reproduced in any form or by any means without permission in writing from Wordware Publishing, Inc.

Printed in the United States of America

ISBN 1-55622-426-5
10 9 8 7 6 5 4 3 2
9410

AutoCAD is a registered trademark of Autodesk, Inc.
Microsoft is a registered trademark and Windows and the Windows Logo are trademarks of Microsoft Corporation.
Other product names mentioned are used for identification purposes only and may be trademarks of their respective companies.

All inquiries for volume purchases of this book should be addressed to Wordware Publishing, Inc., at the above address. Telephone inquiries may be made by calling:

(214) 423-0090

Contents

Hour 1: Setting Up the Drawing 1
   Introduction 1
   Before You Begin 1
   Starting AutoCAD LT 2
   The AutoCAD Window 3
      The Crosshair Cursor 3
      The Menu Bar 4
      The Toolbar 5
      The Toolbox 9
      The Command Area 10
      The Text Window 11
   The Help Window 12
      Context-Sensitive Help 12
      Searching 14
   Preparing for Drawing the Yard 15
      Name the Drawing 15
      Setting the Units 16
      Turning On Snap and Grid 17
      Setting the Limits 18
      Creating New Layers 19
   Saving the Drawing 21

Hour 2: Drawing the Yard Outline 24
   Introduction 24
   Bringing Back the Yard Drawing (File|1) 24
   Drawing the Lot Boundary (Draw|Line) 25
   Changing Layers (Layer) 26
   Drawing the House Outline (Draw|Polyline,
      Assist|Object Snap) 28
   Moving the House into Position (Modify|Move,
      View|Redraw) 31

Adding the Street and Driveway (Construct|Fillet, Construct|Mirror)	33
Putting the Drawing on Paper (File|Print/Plot)	36

Hour 3: Adding Details to the Landscape Plan ... 40

Introduction	40
Dividing the Lot	40
Smoothing the Polyline (Modify|Edit Polyline)	42
Non-Modal Editing	43
Creating the Hatch Boundary	46
Hatching the Lawn (Draw|Hatch)	49
Creating a Symbol (Draw|Circle, Construct|Array)	50
Making a Symbol (Construct|Make Block)	53
Adding Many More Trees (Aerial View, Draw|Insert Block)	54
Drawing the Pond (Pan, Draw|Ellipse, Construct|Offset)	59

Hour 4: Changing the Landscape ... 62

Introduction	62
Changing the Look of Lines (Settings|Linetype, Modify|Change Properties, LtScale)	62
Changing Line Lengths (Modify|Change Points)	65
Changing the Look of the Pond (Modify|Stretch)	66
Measuring the Area of the Lawn (Assist|Area)	70
Adding a Fence (Assist|XYZ Filters, Assist|List, Assist|Dist)	71

Hour 5: Adding Notes and Dimensions ... 76

Introduction	76
Adding a Note to the Drawing (Draw|Text)	76
Changing the Text Font (Settings|Text Style)	78
Changing Existing Text (Modify|Edit Text, Edit|Rotate)	81
A Fast Way to Place Text	84
Reducing Text Display Time (Qtext)	85
Dimensioning the Yard (Dimscale)	86
Horizontal and Continuous Dimensions (Draw|Linear Dimensions)	87

Vertical and Baseline Dimensions	89
Aligned and Radial Dimensions (Draw|Radial Dimensions)	91
Hour 6: Creating Symbols and Attributes	**94**
Introduction	94
Before You Begin	95
Preparing for Drawing the Symbols	95
Selecting the Components	96
Drawing the First Symbol (Draw|Donut)	98
Creating the Attribute Fields (Construct|Define Attribute)	99
Combining the Symbol and Attribute into a Block	103
Storing Blocks on Disk (File|Import/Export|Block Out)	105
Loading Blocks from Disk (File|Import/Export|Wmf In)	106
Creating the Other Blocks	108
Drawing the Electrical Schematic (Draw|Insert Block)	111
Hour 7: Bills of Material	**115**
Introduction	115
Step 1: Create Attribute Extract Template File	116
Step 2: Extract Attribute Data (File|Import/Export|Attributes Out)	116
Step 3: Importing the BOM into Excel	119
Summary	121
Hour 8: Programming AutoCAD Macros	**122**
Introduction	122
Customizing the Toolbar	122
Preprogrammed Macros	125
Changing a Macro	127
Multi-command Macros	129
Summary	131
Appendix A: Setting Up AutoCAD LT for Windows	**132**
Introduction	132
Computer Hardware Requirements	132
Operating System	132
CPU	132

                Memory 132
                Disk Drives 133
                Peripherals 133
         Installing AutoCAD LT for Windows 134
Appendix B: Installing and Using the Bonus Disk 140
         Introduction 140
         DWG Drawing Files 140
         DWG Block and TXT Attribute Files 141
Index 143

Hour 1
SETTING UP THE DRAWING

INTRODUCTION

In this chapter, you learn how to start AutoCAD LT for Windows and set it up in preparation for drawing. You tour the AutoCAD user interface and get your feet wet by drawing a few lines. By the end of the chapter, you know how to save your work to disk and how to get out of AutoCAD.

BEFORE YOU BEGIN

To learn AutoCAD in a day, you work with a drawing based on something you can easily find: the yard. The example used for the two-dimensional drafting portion of this book creates and modifies a drawing of the yard around your home.

Before you begin this tutorial, you may want to measure your yard and locate major features, such as the house, driveway, and garden areas.

Hour 1

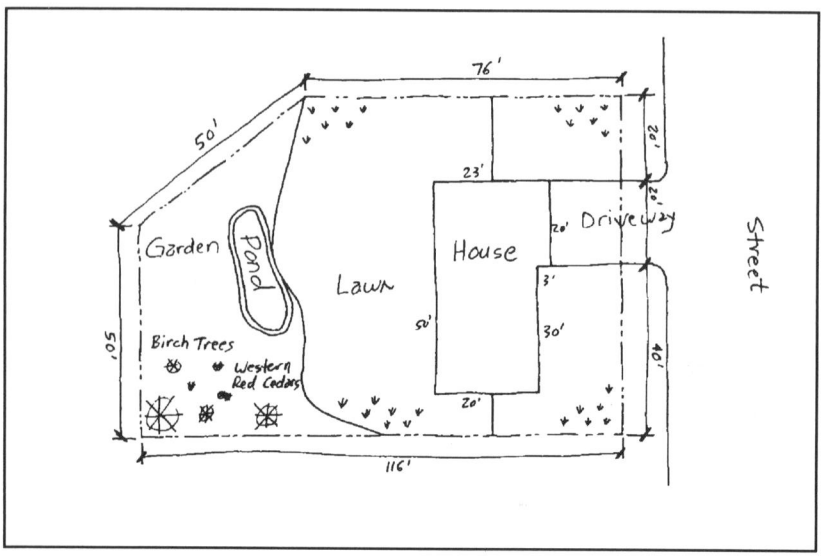

If you'd rather not or if your home doesn't have a yard, you can follow along with the yard sketch above, which is the drawing this book uses.

STARTING AUTOCAD LT

Start Windows by typing at the DOS prompt, as follows:

   C:\> win

When the setup program installed AutoCAD LT on your computer, it created a program group called AutoCAD LT. (If AutoCAD is not yet set up on your computer, read Appendix A, "Setting Up AutoCAD LT for Windows.") Double-click on the AutoCAD LT icon to launch AutoCAD.

Depending on the speed of your computer, it takes from 20 seconds to over a minute to load AutoCAD. While AutoCAD loads, the following copyright notice appears:

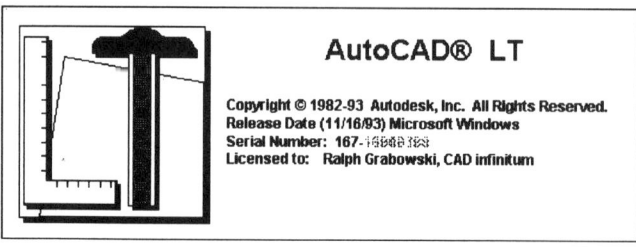

Finally, the AutoCAD LT window appears.

THE AUTOCAD WINDOW

When the AutoCAD LT window appears, it consists of a graphical drawing area with information areas: the title bar, menu bar, and toolbar (along the top) and the command prompt area, at the bottom. In addition, you see the crosshair cursor and the floating toolbox.

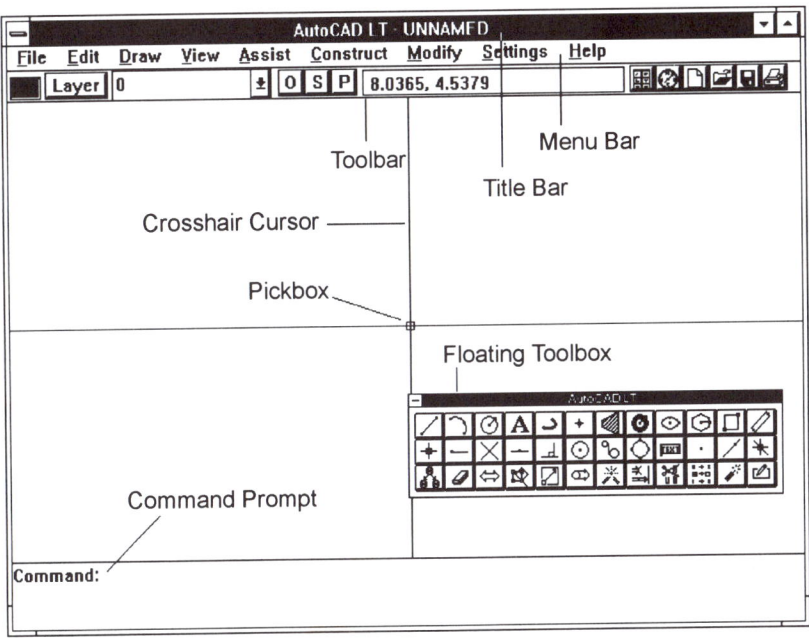

THE CROSSHAIR CURSOR The cursor gives you feedback from AutoCAD. Try moving the cursor around the AutoCAD window by moving your mouse. While in the AutoCAD drawing area, the cursor is a crosshair to show where you are in the drawing. The small box in the center of the crosshairs is called the "pickbox," which shows you the point you are picking. You use the cursor pickbox in Hour 4, "Changing the Landscape."

When you move the crosshair out of the drawing area, the cursor changes to an arrow shape. You are probably familiar with the arrow cursor from other Windows applications. The arrow cursor lets you

Hour 1

make menu selections and pick icon buttons. When the cursor turns to a double-ended arrow, you can resize the window.

THE MENU BAR At the top of the AutoCAD window are three lines of information. From top to bottom, these are:

- Title Bar, which reports the program name and current drawing file name, as in "AutoCAD LT - UNNAMED"
- Menu Bar, as in File, Edit, Draw, etc.
- Toolbar with Layer, O, S, and P buttons

The menu bar is similar to those used by other Windows programs and other versions of AutoCAD. Four of the menu names are identical to those found in other Windows applications: File, Edit, View, and Help. The remaining five are unique to AutoCAD LT: Draw, Assist, Construct, Modify, and Settings.

Try using the menu bar right now:

1. Move your mouse so that the cursor touches the menu bar.
2. Move the mouse left or right until the cursor is over the word **Settings**.
3. Press the first button (the leftmost button on the mouse) to select the Settings menu. Instantly, a menu pops down that lists four of AutoCAD's settings options: Full Menu, Entity Modes, Drawing Aids, and Layer Control. You are seeing a feature of AutoCAD LT that displays short menus to make the menu options less confusing. For this book, we need AutoCAD's complete set of menus.

4. Select the **Full Menu** item to switch from AutoCAD's short-form menus to the full menu system.
5. Now click on **Settings** again. This time a longer menu pops down, listing 16 items. Following are symbols among the menu items that have special meaning.

4

Setting Up the Drawing

Menu Symbol	*Example*	*When Selected...*
(none)	Short Menus	Executes a command
... (ellipsis)	Entity Modes...	Displays a dialog box
▶ (arrow)	Linetype Style ▶	Displays a secondary menu
√ (check)	√ Associative Dimensions	Feature is turned on

6. Click anywhere on the drawing screen to dismiss the menu.

THE TOOLBAR Below the menu bar is the toolbar, consisting of status information and several iconic buttons, as shown below.

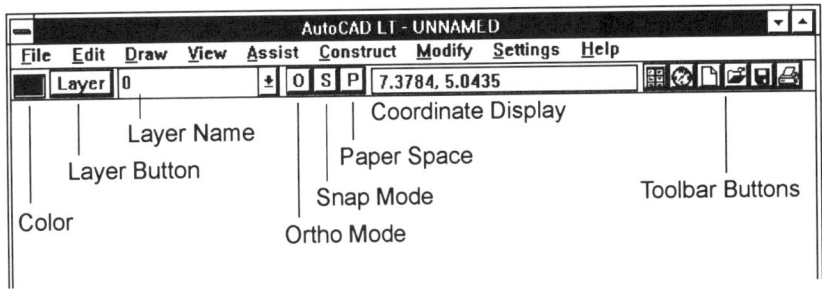

Color Button—The drawing color, currently black. Clicking on the color button displays the Entity Creation Modes dialog box, which lets you set the current color, layer, linetype, text style, elevation, and thickness.

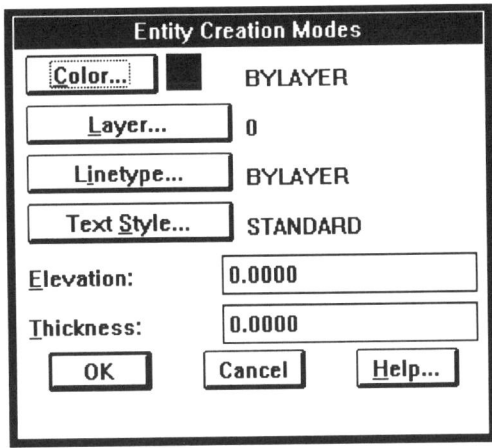

5

Hour 1

To change the working color, click on the dialog box's Color button. This displays the Select Color dialog box. AutoCAD works with 255 colors; select a color by clicking on it, then clicking on the OK buttons until both dialog boxes are gone.

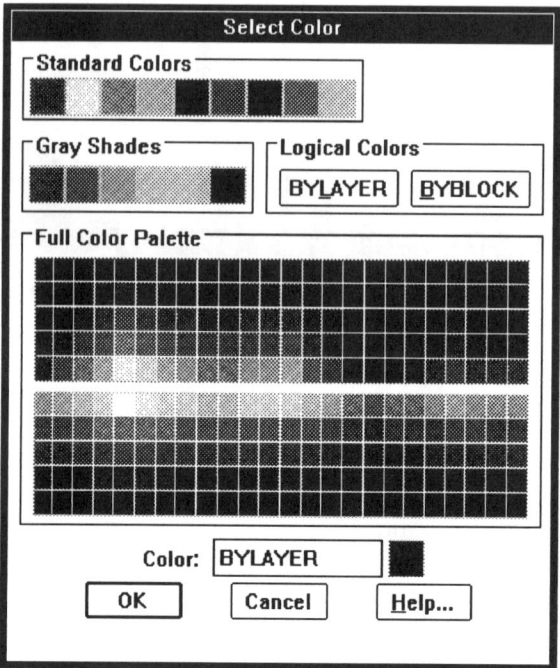

Layer Button—The Layer button displays the current layer name, as in "Layer 0." Clicking on the Layer button displays the Layer Control dialog box, which lets you create and set layer names.

Setting Up the Drawing

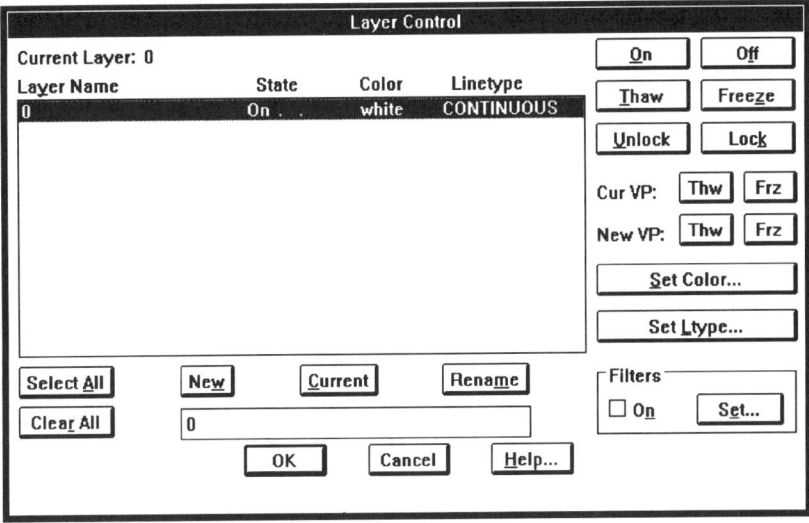

Clicking on the down arrow next to the layer name, 0, displays a list of all layer names in the drawing. A new drawing, such as this one, has only one layer named "0". Selecting a name from the layer list causes AutoCAD to set that layer name as the current layer.

Ortho Mode, Snap Mode, Paper Space—The setting of ortho, snap, and paper space modes, as in "O S P." Clicking on a button makes it look depressed, meaning the mode is turned on. Clicking the button a second time turns the mode off.

Coordinate Display—The current x-, y-coordinates, as in "5.0000, 9.0000". Clicking on the coordinate display changes the display between three modes: static, dynamic, and relative, as described later this hour.

Toolbar Buttons—The status of iconic buttons at the right end of the toolbar. Clicking on a button executes an AutoCAD command or a short macro.

The number of buttons you see depends on the resolution of Windows, the size of the AutoCAD window, and the size of text font selected for the toolbar. The higher the resolution, the more buttons you see (up to a maximum of 26).

7

The buttons predefined by AutoCAD LT have the following meaning:

Icon	Command	Description
Buttons visible at VGA resolution		
	Toolbox	Toggle display and location of the Toolbox
	DsViewer	Toggle display of the Aerial View window
	New	Start a new drawing
	Open	Open an existing drawing
	Save	Save the drawing to disk
	Plot	Print the drawing
	Zoom	Make the drawing appear larger and smaller
	Pan	Move the drawing in the window
Additional buttons visible at Super VGA resolution		
	Redraw	Clean up the screen display
	DdrModes	Display the Entity Creation Modes dialog box
	@	Relative coordinate entry
	.X	X-coordinate filter
	.Y	Y-coordinate filter

Setting Up the Drawing

Icon	Command	Description
Additional buttons visible at Super VGA resolution (Continued)		
◁	Close	Close the line segment
✎	U	Undo the effect of the last command
⊠	Redo	Redo the effect of the U command
Additional button visible at high resolution		
⌘	\3\3	Cancel the current command
Buttons 18 through 26	Not predefined	

You can change the displayed icons, add new icons, and define meaning of the icons. See Hour 8, "Writing Macros for AutoCAD LT."

THE TOOLBOX The toolbox is a collection of 36 icon buttons that floats anywhere on the desktop or sticks to one side of the drawing area. If you don't see the toolbox displayed on the screen, click on the toolbox icon on the toolbar. Each time you click the icon, the toolbox changes location: from stuck to the right side to floating anywhere on the Windows desktop to stuck on the left side.

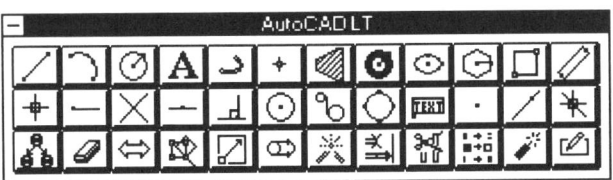

When the toolbox floats, the meaning of the icon is displayed on the toolbox's miniature title bar as you pass the cursor over each icon. You can change the displayed icons, the meaning of the icons, and even the shape of the toolbox. See Hour 8, "Writing Macros for AutoCAD LT."

9

THE COMMAND AREA Along the bottom of the AutoCAD window is the command prompt area. Here you type AutoCAD commands, if you prefer typing to clicking menu selections. Typing the command names is a fast way to draw and edit if you are a touch typist, but it is slow if you aren't.

Here, AutoCAD prompts you for additional information it might need to complete the command. When you see Command prompt:

> Command:

it means AutoCAD is ready for you to type a command name. Try drawing a few lines now:

1. Type the Line command, as follows:
   Command: **line [Enter]**

   Type the word line, then press the Enter key.

2. The prompt changes from "Command:" to "From point:"
   From point:

   AutoCAD is asking you where the line should start from. As you move the mouse, you see the crosshair cursor move about the drawing portion of the screen.

3. Pick a point on the screen by pressing the first button (also known as the "pick button") on your mouse. AutoCAD changes the prompt to read,
   To point:

   and a "rubber band" line stretches from the point you picked as you move the mouse around.

4. Move the mouse some more and press the pick button again. You have drawn your first line in AutoCAD!

Setting Up the Drawing

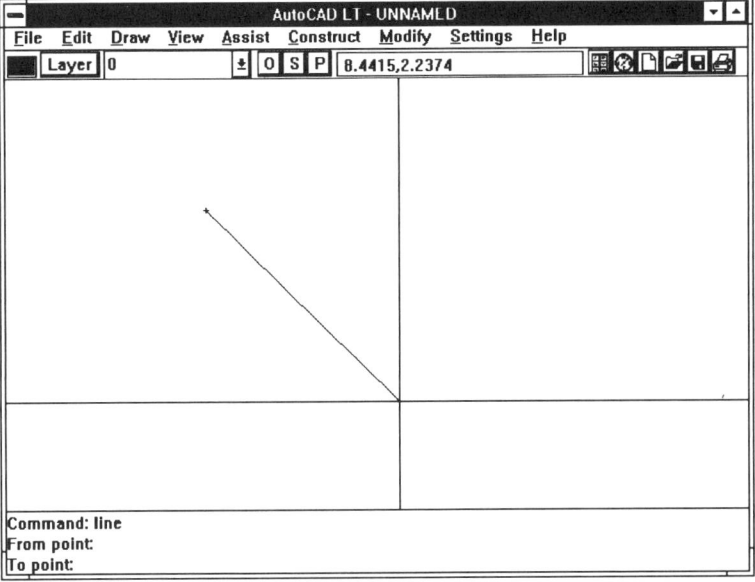

5. Draw another line by moving the mouse and pressing the pick button.
6. You end the Line command by pressing the Enter key, or pressing Ctrl+C, or pressing the rightmost mouse button, as follows:

   To point: **[Enter]**

   Pressing Ctrl+C cancels any AutoCAD command; some commands may need a couple of Ctrl+C presses.
7. To erase the lines you drew, type u at the command prompt to undo the lines, as follows:

   Command: **u**

THE TEXT WINDOW If you need to see more than three lines of the command prompt area, you can switch to the text screen by pressing function key F2. Instantly, a second AutoCAD window appears on the screen, labeled "AutoCAD LT Text."

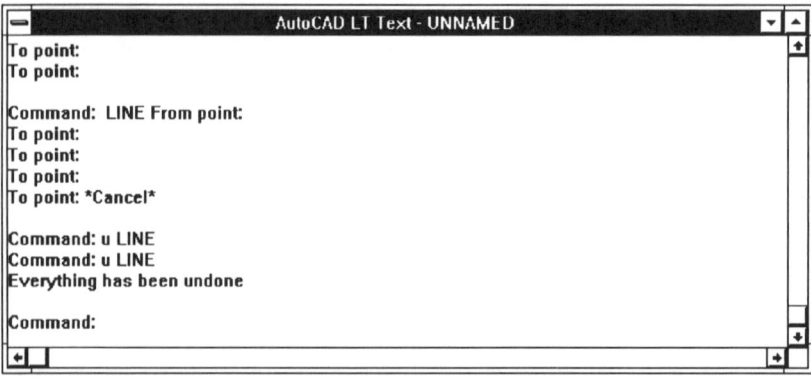

The text screen displays the most recent 1,500 lines of text. You scroll back to earlier text by clicking on the vertical scroll bar at the right edge of the window.

You return to the graphics screen by pressing F2 again. F2 is called the "flipscreen" key.

THE HELP WINDOW

AutoCAD's on-line help system is similar to that of most other Windows applications. At any time, you call up Help on AutoCAD LT as follows:

1. Select **Help|Contents**. The vertical bar (|) is shorthand for the following actions: click on the menu bar's **Help** item, then select **Contents** from the pop-down menu.
2. Click on **Basic Procedures** and a list of topics titled "Getting Started with AutoCAD LT" appears.
3. Click on any green underlined word to find out more about a topic. In the Help window, any word underlined and printed in a green color is "hot-linked" to related topics.
4. To get back to the main contents, click on the **Contents** button.

CONTEXT-SENSITIVE HELP The AutoCAD LT Help system is context-sensitive. That means Help displays helpful information related to the current AutoCAD command as follows:

Setting Up the Drawing

1. Type the Line command, then press F1. Pressing F1 invokes context-sensitive help, as follows:

   Command: **line**
   From point: **[F1]** '_help
   Resuming LINE command
   From point:

   AutoCAD displays helpful information about using the Line command.

   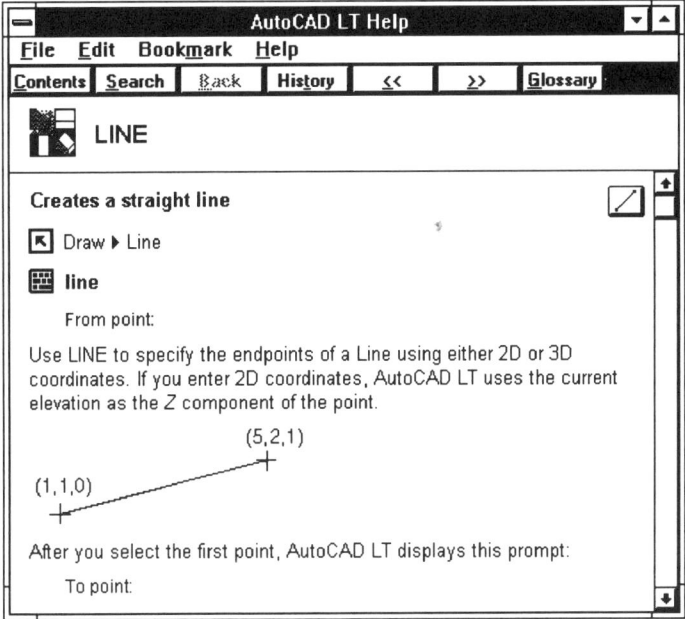

2. As you move the cursor about the Help text, it sometimes changes from the arrow to a pointing finger. When the finger appears, click the mouse button and the definition of the word or icon is displayed in a box.
3. Click anywhere to dismiss the definition box.
4. Click **File|Exit** on the AutoCAD LT Help menu to close the Help window. Press Ctrl+C to end the Line command.

   Resuming LINE command
   From point: **Ctrl+C**
   Command:

Hour 1

SEARCHING You can search for the meaning of a particular aspect of AutoCAD LT as follows:

1. Select **Help|Search for Help on...** from within AutoCAD or click on the **Search** button within the Help window. The Search dialog box appears.

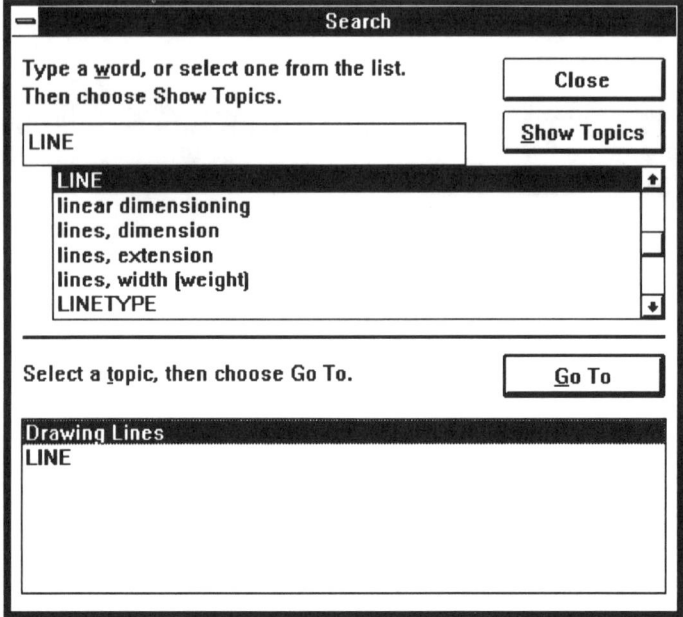

2. Type the word you are searching for in the text box, such as "LINE."
3. Click on the **Search** button. A list of related topics appears at the bottom of the dialog box.
4. Select a topic at the bottom, such as "Drawing Lines."
5. Finally, click on the **Go To** button and information on drawing lines appears.
6. Exit the Help window by selecting **File|Exit**.

Now that you are familiar with the AutoCAD window and its Help system, you can go ahead and set up the drawing environment.

Setting Up the Drawing

PREPARING FOR DRAWING THE YARD

Before you draw the yard, you need to prepare AutoCAD for a new drawing. For the remainder of this first hour, you learn how to name the drawing; set the units, snap, and grid; set the limits; and name the layers.

NAME THE DRAWING Give a new drawing its own name as follows:

1. Select **File|New**. Because you've already drawn some lines in the Unnamed drawing, AutoCAD displays the following dialog box.

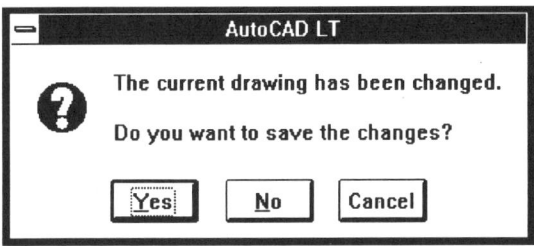

2. Click the No button to discard the changes and AutoCAD displays the Create New Drawing dialog box.

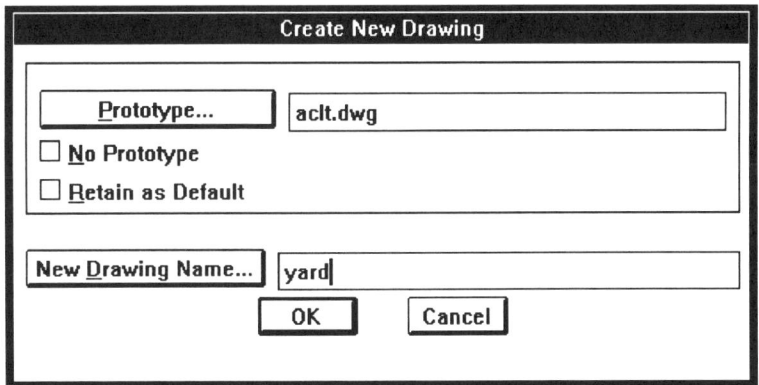

3. Type **yard** in the text box next to New Drawing Name and click on the **OK** button. At the bottom of all dialog boxes are two buttons:

15

- OK exits the dialog box with the changes you made
- Cancel exits the dialog box and discards the changes you made

AutoCAD saves the drawing in the current subdirectory with the name "yard.dwg" and removes the dialog box. From now on, you and AutoCAD refer to this drawing as "yard."

SETTING THE UNITS AutoCAD displays units in a variety of measurement styles, such as fractional, decimal, and exponential. Once you set a measurement style, AutoCAD expects to read all input from you in that style; AutoCAD also displays all measurements in that style of units.

1. Select **Settings|Units Style**. (Recall that the vertical bar, |, separates menu picks: pick **Settings** from the menu bar and, when the pop-down menu appears, select **Units Style**.) AutoCAD displays the Units Control dialog box.

2. On the left are the five forms of units AutoCAD works with. When you measured your yard, you probably measured the distances in feet, inches, and fractional inches. For this reason, you should pick the circle (called a "radio button") next to Architectural. If you measured your yard in meters and centimeters, you would pick the radio button next to Decimal.

3. Below Units is the Precision list box. Measurements to the nearest 1/4-inch are accurate enough for this project. Click on the down arrow and select the **0'-0 1/4"** item. (If necessary, click on

Setting Up the Drawing

the vertical scroll bar until 0'-0 1/4" is visible.) You still enter distances more accurately than 1/4-inch because AutoCAD remembers the distance to full accuracy. However, AutoCAD displays coordinates and reports distances to the nearest 1/4-inch.

4. The dialog box also controls the display and orientation of angles and bearings in a drawing. On the right of the dialog box are the five kinds of angles AutoCAD works with. By default, AutoCAD uses the Cartesian method of measuring angles:

- Fractional degrees are measured in decimals.
- 0 degrees is to the east (the positive x-direction).
- Positive angles are measured counterclockwise.

If we were real land surveyors, we would change fractional degrees to minutes and seconds. The Direction... button brings up a second dialog box that lets you change the 0-degree orientation to North and measure positive angles clockwise. However, AutoCAD's method of angle measurement is so pervasive that we retain the default values for the purpose of learning AutoCAD in a day.

5. When you finish setting the units, pick the **OK** button.

TURNING ON SNAP AND GRID One great advantage to drawing with a computer is that it allows you to create very accurate drawings. AutoCAD has several features that help you draw with perfect accuracy. One is called "snap" mode; you learn about others later in the book. AutoCAD's snap can be thought of as setting a drawing resolution.

1. Select **Settings|Drawing Aids**. AutoCAD displays the Drawing Aids dialog box.

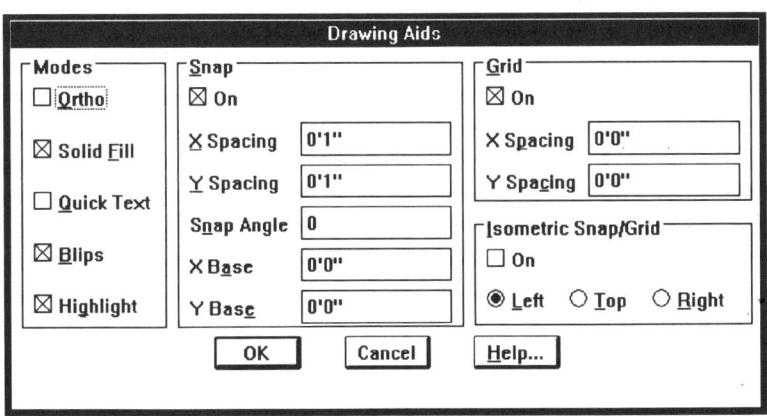

17

2. To draw everything to an accuracy of one inch, click on the square (called the "check box") next to **On** under the word **Snap**. AutoCAD LT comes preset for 1" snap distance in the x and y directions.

3. As a visual guide, turn on a grid (an array of dots) by clicking the **On** check box under the word **Grid**. A grid distance of 0'0" means that the grid spacing matches the snap spacing, 1" in our case.

4. Click on **OK**. The dialog box disappears and the drawing area is filled with an array of grid dots spaced 1 inch apart.

5. Move your mouse around and note how the cursor jumps on the screen instead of moving smoothly. The cursor is jumping in 1-inch increments. Look at the coordinate display and notice it is changing by the nearest inch, rather than the nearest 1/4-inch as set earlier.

SETTING THE LIMITS There is no practical limit to the size of drawing you can create with AutoCAD. You could draw the entire solar system full-size if you wanted. The Limits command is useful for showing the nominal limits of a drawing and for constraining the limits of the grid marks. By specifying the lower left and upper right coordinates, you constrain the limits of the grid marks and the display of the Zoom All command.

Take a look at the sketch of your yard. Leaving about 20 feet of "breathing room" around the edges of the example drawing, work out the dimensions of the limits. Assume that the lower left corner of the yard is located at (0,0).

1. Select **Settings|Drawing|Limits**. AutoCAD prompts you to enter the coordinates of the lower left and upper right corners, as follows:

   Command: _limits
   Reset Model space limits:
   ON/OFF/<Lower left corner> <0'-0",0'-0">: **-20',-20'**
   Upper right corner <1'-0",0'-9">: **140',100'**

Don't forget to type the apostrophes ('), which tell AutoCAD you are entering measurements in feet.

2. Now use the Zoom All command to see the extents of the drawing limits, as follows:

   Command: **zoom**
   All/Center/Extents/Previous/Window/<Scale(X/XP)>: **a**
   Regenerating drawing.
   Grid too dense to display

For most of AutoCAD's command options, you only need to type the first letter of the option. Here you type "a" as the abbreviation for the "All" option.

Previously, AutoCAD displayed an area 1 foot by 9 inches; now AutoCAD displays 160 feet by 120 feet. Thus, the Zoom command lets you see the "big picture" as well as zooming in for a detailed look.

3. The grid dots disappear as AutoCAD displays the larger area. Since the grid is meant to guide you—not to get in your way or disappear—change the spacing to 10 feet by repeating **Settings|Drawing Aids**.
4. When the Drawing Aids dialog box appears, change the value of the grid's x-spacing to **10'**.
5. Click on the **OK** button. The grid reappears spaced 10 feet apart (AutoCAD automatically set the grid's y-spacing to 10'.)

CREATING NEW LAYERS If you have worked with overlay drafting, then you are familiar with the concept of layers. In overlay drafting, you draw the base plan on one mylar sheet, the electrical on another sheet, and the structural on a third. Since the mylar is transparent, you can overlay the three drawings to create a single blueprint.

Layers in CAD operate in a similar manner. You draw parts of the drawing on different layers. Then, you turn layers off and on to display the drawing in different ways. For example, the electrical contractor might be interested in seeing only the base plan layer and the electrical layer.

AutoCAD lets you use layer names up to 31 characters long, effectively giving you an unlimited number of layers in a drawing. The easiest way to set up layer names is with AutoCAD's Layer button.

Hour 1

1. Move the mouse to the toolbar and click on the **Layer** button. AutoCAD displays the Layer Control dialog box. The dialog box lets you control almost every aspect of AutoCAD's layers. As you can see, the only layer currently in the drawing is a layer called "0." Every new AutoCAD drawing has this one layer.

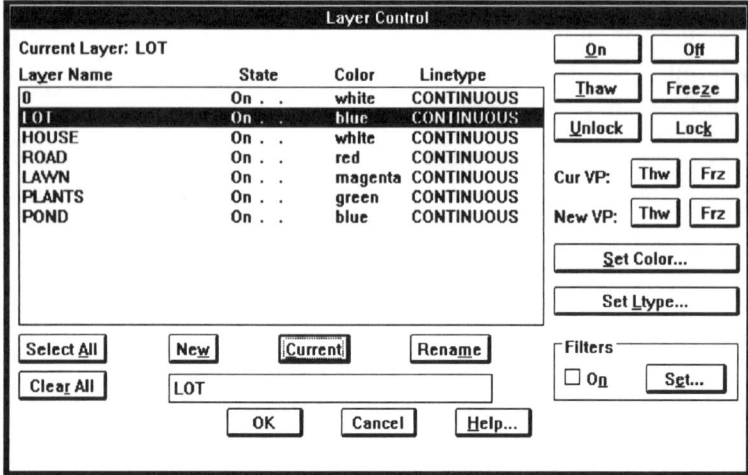

2. Create a layer by typing the first layer name, **Lot**, in the text box below the New button.
3. Click on the **New** button and AutoCAD adds "Lot" to the list of layer names.
4. If you have a color display, you may want to assign a color to each layer. This makes it easy to determine which lines belong to which layer. Change the color of the Lot layer to blue by picking layer name **Lot**, then the **Set Color** button (located on the right side of the dialog box). A second dialog box appears called Select Color.
5. The Select Color dialog box displays 255 different colors or 15 colors repeated over 16 times, depending on the capabilities of your computer's graphics board. Pick the blue box under Standard Colors, at the top of the dialog box. The word "Blue" appears next to the Color text box at the bottom of the dialog box.
6. Click on the **OK** button to exit the Select Color dialog box. The name of the color next to layer Lot changes to "blue."
7. Click on the **Clear All** button.

Setting Up the Drawing

8. Add the remaining layer names and colors, using the following table as a guide:

Layer Name	Layer Color
House	white
Road	red
Lawn	magenta (pink)
Plants	green
Pond	blue

9. When you finish, pick the **Lot** layer name, then the **Current** button. All drawing from now on occurs on the Lot layer.
10. To exit the Layer Control dialog box, click on the **OK** button at the bottom of the dialog box.
11. Notice how the name of the layer on the toolbar changed from "0" to "LOT."

SAVING THE DRAWING

Let's review the drawing to this point. Although you haven't drawn anything yet, the drawing file contains a fair amount of information.

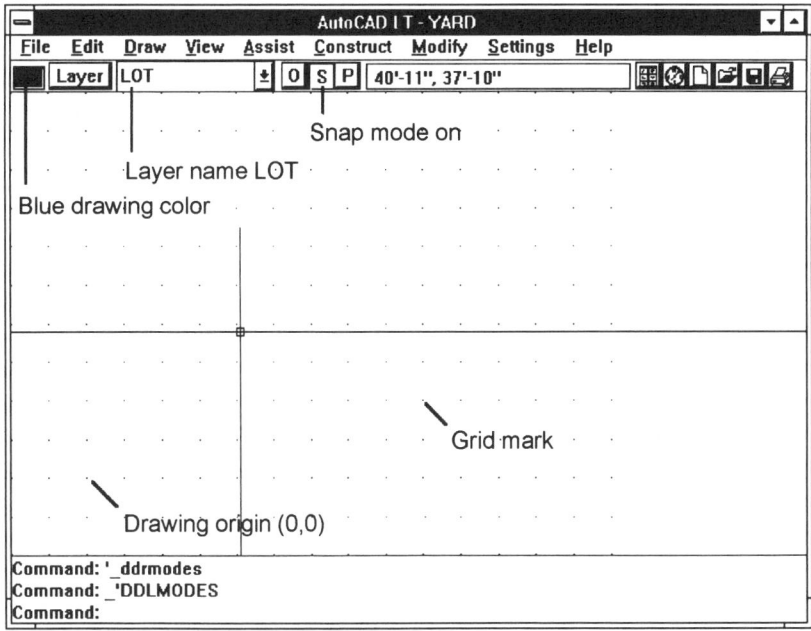

21

Hour 1

On the status line, you see the color of the current layer is blue and its name is Lot. You also see that snap mode is turned on, that the coordinates are displaying in feet and inches, and the grid is turned on. The preceding figure also shows you where the origin (0,0) is located. In the next chapter, you begin drawing the lot from the origin.

For speed, AutoCAD keeps the drawing in the computer's memory. The drawback is that if Windows crashes your computer or if the power is cut, you lose your work. Since Windows crashes are common, it is a good idea to save your drawing every ten or fifteen minutes.

1. You save your drawing to disk with the **Save** command. Click on the diskette icon (the fifth icon on the toolbar). AutoCAD saves the drawing to disk.

2. AutoCAD lets you set a time to automatically save the drawing without using the Save command. The default setting is turned off, which doesn't do any good. Turn on the automatic save feature by selecting **File|Preferences**. AutoCAD displays the Preferences dialog box.

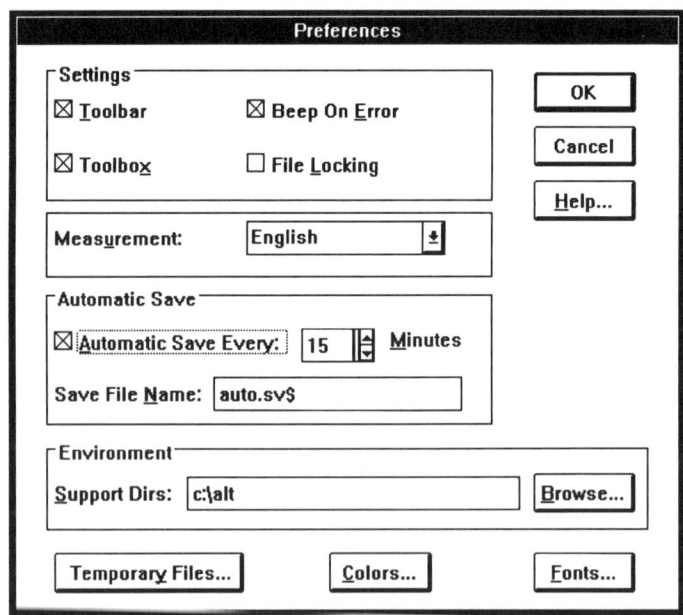

3. Click on the check box next to **Automatic Save Every**. AutoCAD saves the drawing every fifteen minutes to a file called auto.sv$. Even though AutoCAD now automatically saves the drawing, it is still a good idea for you to save your work after finishing any amount of editing and drawing.
4. Look over the Preferences dialog box. You might want to turn off **File Locking**, turn off the **Toolbox**, and turn on **Beep on Error**. An "X" in the check box means the feature is turned on.
5. Click on **OK**.
6. If you need to take a break at this point, use **File|Exit** to leave AutoCAD. AutoCAD closes its window and you find yourself back at the Windows Program Manager.

In the next chapter, you begin drawing the yard with AutoCAD based on the sketch you created earlier—or based on the example given in this book. You also learn how to make simple changes and print out a copy of the drawing on your printer.

Hour 2

DRAWING THE YARD OUTLINE

INTRODUCTION

In the first hour, you learned how to start AutoCAD, set up a new drawing, and save the drawing to the computer's hard disk. This hour, you learn how to draw accurate lines, make simple changes to the drawing, and produce a copy of the drawing on your printer.

BRINGING BACK THE YARD DRAWING (File|1)

If you exited AutoCAD at the end of the last hour, you need to restart AutoCAD and load the Yard drawing.

1. Make sure Windows is running. Load AutoCAD by double-clicking on the AutoCAD LT icon.
2. When the AutoCAD LT window appears, select **File|1 YARD**. Recall that the vertical bar, |, separates menu picks: pick **File** from the menu bar, then select **1 YARD** from the pop-down menu.

AutoCAD LT remembers the last four drawings you worked with and displays their names at the bottom of the **File** popdown menu. When you select one of the four drawing names, AutoCAD executes the **Open**

command and loads the drawing. It should look exactly the same as when you last saw the drawing.

DRAWING THE LOT BOUNDARY (Draw|Line)

Let's get some lines on the screen! To orient yourself, the first thing you should draw is the boundary of the yard. The lines making up the lot boundary are drawn with the Line command.

1. Begin drawing the lot lines at the lower left corner, the origin (0,0). Select **Draw|Line** and respond to the prompts, as follows:
   Command: _line From point: **0,0**

AutoCAD prints "_line" to confirm your selection of the Line command.

2. To draw the lower 116'-long boundary line, you know that the other end of the line must be located at coordinate (116',0):
   To point: **116',0**

3. The next line is 80 feet north, which is coordinate (116',80'):
   To point: **116',80'**

4. You drew the first two lines with absolute coordinates, where you calculated the coordinates based on your measurements. However, AutoCAD can do the calculations for you. When you use "relative coordinates," AutoCAD draws a line from the current point based on the length and direction you specify. Continue drawing the lot boundary using relative coordinates, as follows:
   To point: **@76'<180**
   To point: **@50'<216.88**

When you tell AutoCAD to draw a line with relative coordinates, you use a special notation that has the following meaning:

Notation	Meaning
@	Use relative coordinates
76'	Distance is 76 feet from the current point
<	Draw the line at an angle...
180	...of 180 degrees

25

Hour 2

Although the line is drawn relative to the current point, the angle is measured in absolute degrees, using the East-is-0-degrees convention. Using relative coordinates makes sense when you have many angled lines to draw.

5. To finish the lot boundary, you use a shortcut. Type "c" (short for "close") instead of typing the final coordinates (0,0), as follows:

   To point: **c**

AutoCAD automatically draws a line from the current endpoint to the beginning of the first line.

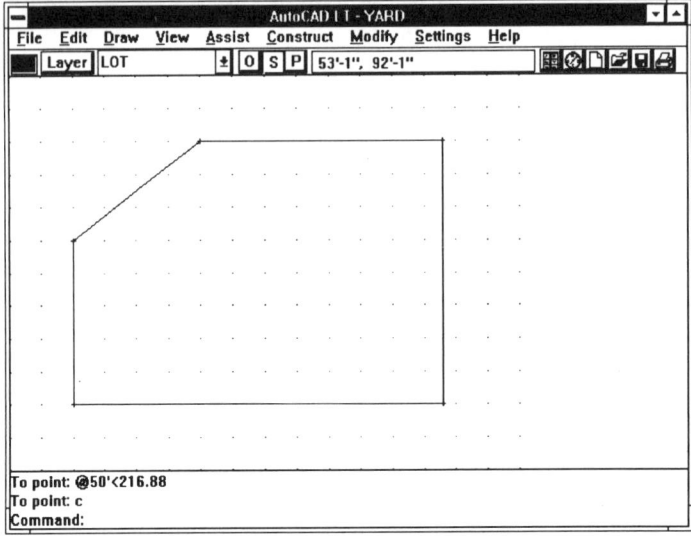

Instead of drafting on paper, you have created your first electronic drawing! More important, you have drawn it full size. That's one of the powerful aspects of CAD. There is no need to use a scale ruler or divide distances by a scaling factor. Everything is drawn full size.

CHANGING LAYERS (Layer)

From the sketch, you know that the lower right corner of the house is located 10' up and 20' in from the lot corner. There are several ways to locate the corner of the house: (1) draw a pair of construction lines 10' and 20' long and erase them later; (2) calculate the coordinates of the corner; or (3) draw the house in the corner of the lot and then move the house into position. You'll use the third method to exercise two of AutoCAD's most powerful commands, PLine and Move.

Before you draw the house, you need to change to the layer called "House." Many of AutoCAD LT's commands, including the Layer command, can be carried out in more than one way (in up to six different ways, by my count). The flexibility lets you choose the method that suits the way you prefer to work.

The six ways to invoke a command in AutoCAD LT are:

- Use the pop-down menus and dialog boxes
- Select an icon button from the toolbar or toolbox
- Type the name at the Command: prompt
- Invoke a script
- Abbreviate the command as an alias via the Aclt.Pgp file
- Program buttons on the mouse

In the first hour, you used the Layer Control dialog box to create new layers and set the Lot layer. This time, try typing the word "layer" at the Command: prompt.

1. To set the House layer, type the Layer command, as follows:
   Command: **layer**

2. The Layer command presents you with 12 options, most of which you ignore for now, as follows:
   ?/Make/Set/New/ON/OFF/Color/LType/Freeze/Thaw/LOck/Unlock: **s**

For some commands, AutoCAD presents a list of options. To select an option you need only type its first character, such as M for the Make option and S for the Set option. If two (or more) options begin with the same first letter—such as the LType and LOck options—you may need to type in the first two or three characters (LT and LO). AutoCAD shows you the minimum number of characters by capitalizing them. Type the letter "s" to invoke the Set option.

3. AutoCAD prompts you to enter the name of the layer, as follows:
   New current layer <LOT>: **house**

Notice that AutoCAD lists the current layer name in angle brackets, <LOT>. This is called the "default" name, which lets you retain the current layer by simply pressing the Enter key. To change the working layer to House, type **house** and press **Enter**.

Hour 2

4. The Layer command repeats its 12-option prompt. Press Enter to cancel the command and return to the Command: prompt.
   ?/Make/Set/New/ON/OFF/Color/Ltype/Freeze/Thaw/LOck/Unlock:
   [Enter]
   Command:

You cancel a command at any time by pressing Ctrl+C. Hold down the Ctrl key, type C, then release Ctrl. You may need to press Ctrl+C two or even three times for some commands that have a large number of options, such as the PEdit and Dim commands.

5. Look at the status line to confirm that AutoCAD has changed the working layer from Layer "LOT" to Layer "HOUSE."

DRAWING THE HOUSE OUTLINE
(Draw|Polyline, Assist|Object Snap)

When you drew the lot boundary with the Line command, you created what looks like a continuous line. In fact, each line segment is an independent entity.

To remedy this, AutoCAD has a special type of line called the "polyline." As the prefix "poly" suggests, a polyline is a line made up of many features—lines, arcs, varying widths—all connected together as a single object.

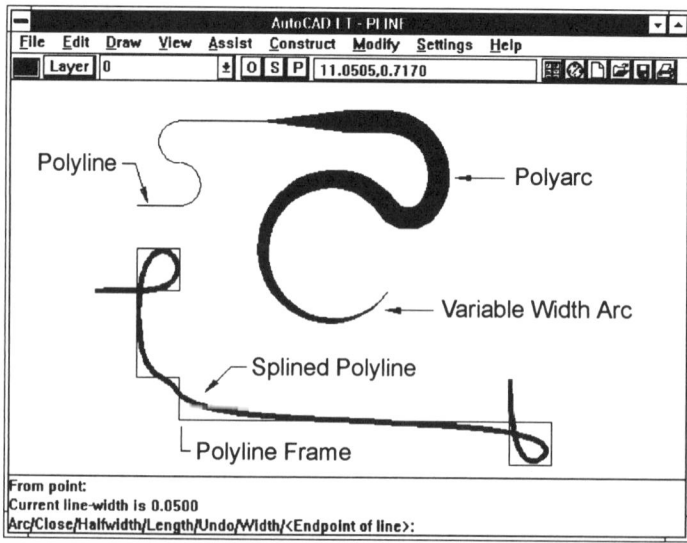

28

1. Draw the house outline as a polyline. Select **Draw|Polyline**. As with the Line command, AutoCAD prompts you for the point from which to begin drawing the polyline:

   Command: _pline
   From point: **int**
   of: **[pick lower right corner of lot]**

2. Instead of specifying a coordinate, you ask AutoCAD to find a geometric feature by using "object snap." When you type "int" (short for intersection) AutoCAD attempts to snap to the nearest intersection, rather than snapping to the nearest 1" you specified with the Snap command in Hour 1. Since the Int snap overrides the 1" snap, this is sometimes referred to as "object snap override."

AutoCAD has ten geometric object snaps:

Mode	Object Snap	Meaning
cen	CENter	center of arc or circle
end	ENDpoint	end of line or arc
ins	INSertion point	of block or text
int	INTersection	intersection of lines, arcs, circle
mid	MIDpoint	middle of line or arc
nea	NEArest	nearest point
nod	NODe	point
per	PERpendicular	perpendicular to line, arc, circle
qua	QUAdrant	0-, 90-, 180-, 270-degree on circle
tan	TANgent	tangent to line, arc, or circle

You use some of the other object snap modes later.

When you type "int," a square appears around the crosshair cursor. The square is called the "object snap aperture" and shows the area in which AutoCAD hunts for the intersection.

3. AutoCAD then curtly prompts you with "of." It is asking you to position the aperture cursor near the intersection of the two lines. Move the mouse until the aperture is over the lower right corner of the lot boundary and press the pick button.

Hour 2

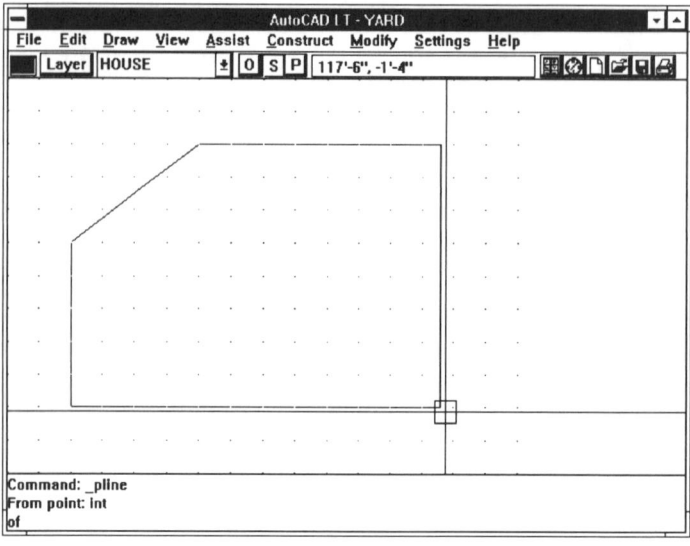

4. AutoCAD then displays a long prompt:

   Current line-width is 0'-0"
   Arc/Close/Halfwidth/Length/Undo/Width/<Endpoint of line>: **@30'<90**

The prompt reports that the polyline currently has no width (0'-0"). That doesn't mean the line is invisible. Rather, "zero width" in CAD means that the line is drawn as narrow as possible on the screen and by the printer.

The second line of the prompt displays seven of the PLine command's 22 options. Don't let it intimidate you; for now, you ignore all except the default, <Endpoint of line>.

5. Draw the remainder of the house outline, as follows:

   Arc/.../<Endpoint of line>: **@3'<0**
   Arc/.../<Endpoint of line>: **@20'<90**
   Arc/.../<Endpoint of line>: **@28'<180**
   Arc/.../<Endpoint of line>: **@50'<270**
   Arc/.../<Endpoint of line>: **c**

You complete the polyline with the C option, as you did with the Line command.

Drawing the Yard Outline

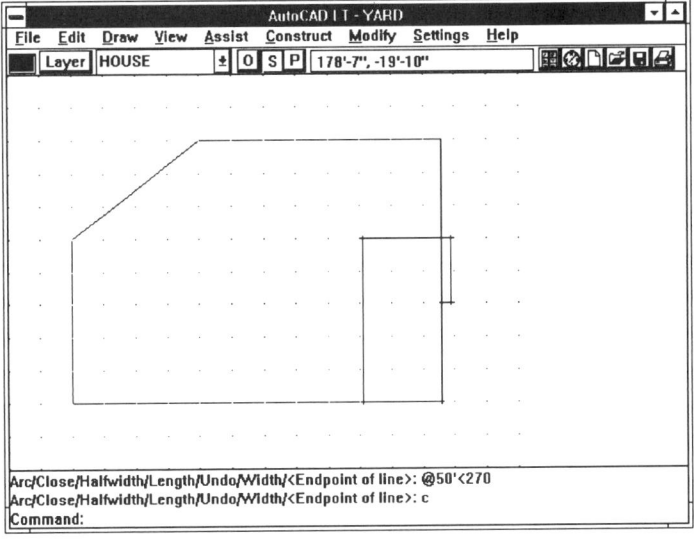

In Hour 1, you had set the color for the House layer to black. Because you changed the layer to House, AutoCAD automatically drew the lines in black instead of blue when Lot was the working layer. If you need, you change colors "on the fly" with the Color command.

MOVING THE HOUSE INTO POSITION
(Modify|Move, View|Redraw)

Now that you've drawn the outline of the house, you move it into position.

1. Select **Modify|Move**. When you start the command, AutoCAD asks you what you want to move, as follows:

   Command: _move
   Select objects: **[pick house]**

AutoCAD changes the crosshair cursor into a small square cursor, called the "pick cursor." Move the cursor to any part of the polyline making up the outline of the house and press the pick button. The entire house outline is "highlighted." The highlighting shows as a dotted line. This is AutoCAD's way of letting you know it found the object you picked.

31

Hour 2

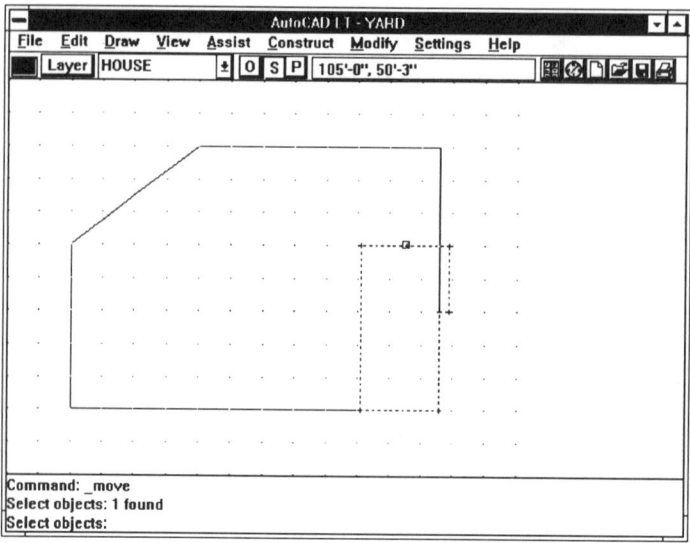

2. AutoCAD lets you select more than one object to move:
   Select objects: **[Enter]**

However, you only need to move the one polyline. Pressing Enter ended the selection process.

3. As in drawing a line, the Move command needs to know a from-point and a to-point. The Move command calls the from-point the "base point," as follows:
   Base point or displacement: **0,0**

4. Now AutoCAD wants to know where you want to move the selected objects. The Move command calls the to-point the "second point," as follows:
   Second point or displacement: **-20',10'**

The coordinates of (-20',10') tell AutoCAD that you want the house moved left by 20 feet (X = -20') and up by 10 feet (Y = 10'). AutoCAD instantly relocates the house. The Move command shows you a powerful aspect of CAD: no eraser dust!

5. The lot boundary probably has a portion missing due to the house moving. You repair the boundary with the **View|Redraw** command. The Redraw command cleans up the screen by redrawing the background and all objects. The screen flashes briefly as AutoCAD completely redraws the drawing.

ADDING THE STREET AND DRIVEWAY
(Construct|Fillet, Construct|Mirror)

The final drafting you do this hour is of the driveway and the street. Before you begin drawing them, change to the Road layer, as follows:

1. Click on the down arrow next to the **House** layer name on the toolbar.
2. When the list box appears, click on **Road**. AutoCAD changes the layer name from House to Road and the working color from black to red.

With the Road layer set, you draw the driveway and street outlines. First you draw the upper roadwork; later you duplicate the lower driveway and street outline with a single command.

3. Select **Draw|Line** to draw the upper driveway and street outline, as follows:

   Command: _line
   From point: **int**
   of: **[pick upper right corner of house]**
   To point: **@28'<0**
   To point: **@40'<90**
   To point: **[Enter]**

4. If you leave out the apostrophe ('), such as 40 instead of 40', the line is drawn only 40 inches long. You can back up and undraw the incorrect line with the "u" option (short for "undo"), as follows:

   To point: **@40<0**
   To point: **u**
   To point: **@40'<0**

5. To add the curb return (the arc joining the driveway and street) use AutoCAD's Fillet command. Fillet draws an arc between two intersecting lines. The lines don't have to physically meet; AutoCAD takes care of extending the lines so that the arc is drawn between them. Unfortunately, you have to use the Fillet command twice: once to set the radius of the arc then again to create the fillet. Select **Construct|Fillet**, as follows:

   Command: _fillet
   Polyline/Radius/<Select two objects>: **r**
   Enter fillet radius <0'-0">: **3'**

33

Hour 2

6. With the fillet radius set at three feet, repeat the Fillet command to perform the actual filleting, as follows:

   Command: **[Enter]**
   FILLET Polyline/Radius/<Select two objects>: **[pick driveway line]**
   Second object: **[pick street line]**

By pressing the Enter key at the Command: prompt, you repeat the previous command, the Fillet command in this case. This AutoCAD feature lets you quickly repeat the command several times.

AutoCAD automatically shortens the two lines to fit the 3-foot arc between them.

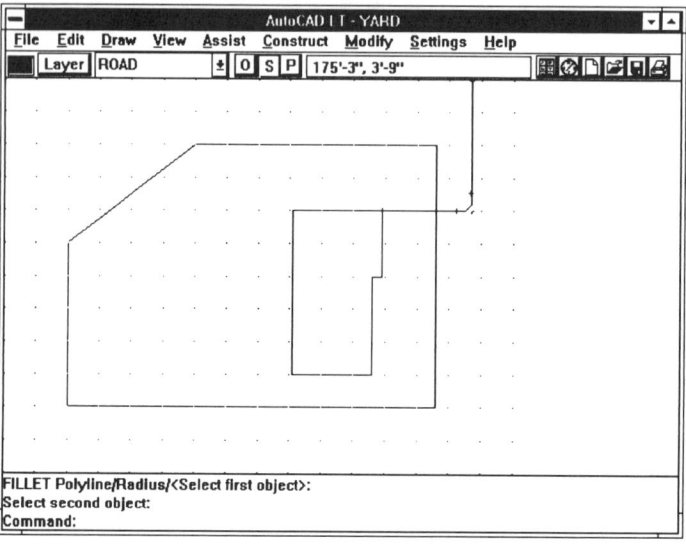

You needed to use the Line command and two applications of the Fillet command to create the part of the driveway and street. One of the most important concepts behind computer-aided anything is that you should never have to draw the same line twice. To illustrate the power of this concept, use the Mirror command to duplicate the lower driveway and street line *without having to draw them!* The Mirror command creates a mirrored copy of a set of objects.

5. Select **Construct|Mirror**. AutoCAD asks you to select the objects you want to mirror, as follows:

   Command: _mirror
   Select objects: **[pick the driveway line]**

Select objects: **[pick the curb return]**
Select objects: **[pick the street line]**
Select objects: **[Enter]**

6. AutoCAD needs you to specify an imaginary line about which it mirrors the objects you just picked:

   First point of mirror line: **mid**
   of: **[pick center of garage entrance]**
   Second point: **per**
   of: **[pick right-hand lot boundary]**

The length of the mirror line is not important but the angle is crucial. For this reason you used two new object snap modes: "mid" to find the midpoint of the garage entrance, and "per" to ensure the mirror line is perpendicular to the lot boundary, as shown.

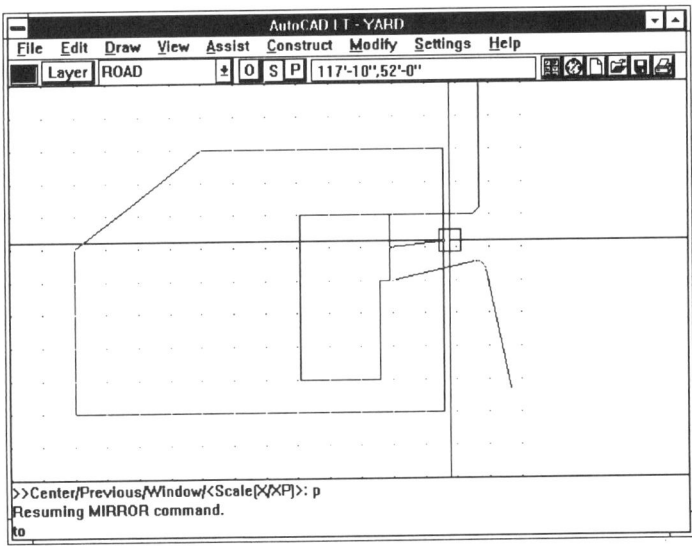

8. At this point, AutoCAD gives you the option of erasing the old objects, the two lines and arc you picked. In most cases, as in this one, you don't want them erased:

   Delete old objects? <N> **n**

AutoCAD draws the lower driveway and street outline as a perfect mirror image of the upper set, as shown in the following figure.

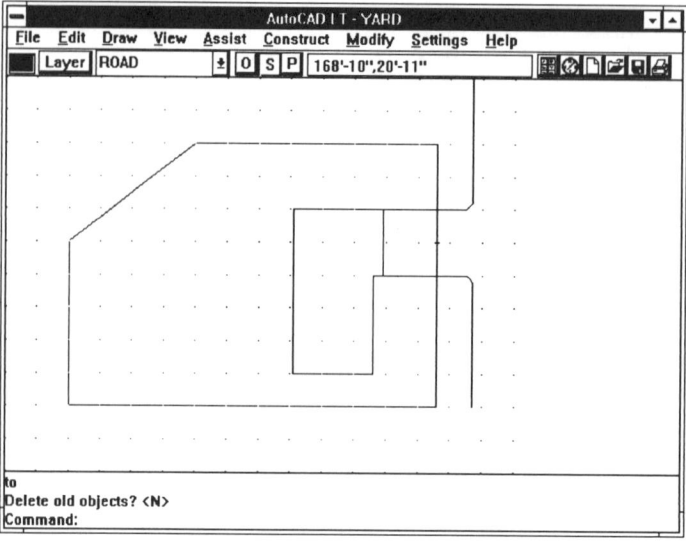

You have now drawn the outline of the lot, house, and roadways. The work you have done is valuable and it is important that you save the drawing to disk. Use the Save button on the toolbar (the miniature picture of the diskette) to store the yard drawing on disk.

PUTTING THE DRAWING ON PAPER (File|Print/Plot)

While it is more efficient (and environmentally aware) to create and store a drawing on a computer, you may want to print a copy of the drawing on paper. That lets you mark up the drawing with notes or show off your progress to your friends!

AutoCAD LT has one command to output the drawing on paper. The Plot command sends the drawing to the Windows default printer. The following series of dialog boxes assumes you have a laser printer compatible with the Hewlett-Packard LaserJet attached to your computer. The commands and prompts for other printers and plotters may differ slightly.

1. Select **File|Print/Plot** to create a check plot of the Yard drawing. AutoCAD displays the Plot Configuration dialog box.

Drawing the Yard Outline

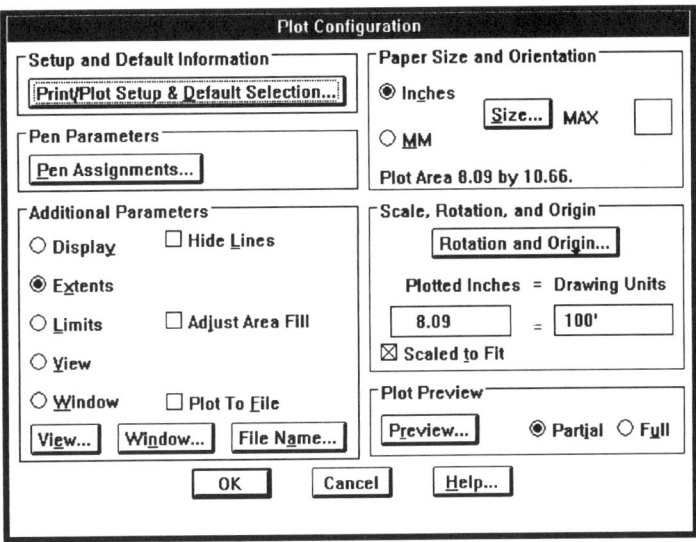

2. The Plot Configuration dialog box has a confusing array of options. For a check plot, you ignore nearly all of them. Click on the radio button next to **Extents** (along the left side, under Additional Parameters). The Extents option ensures that everything in your drawing is plotted on the paper.

3. To quickly check how the drawing fits the paper, click on the **Preview...** button (at the lower right, under Plot Preview). A second dialog box, called Preview Effective Plotting Area, appears on the screen. The red rectangle shows the plotable area of the paper; the blue rectangle shows the extents of the drawing.

37

Hour 2

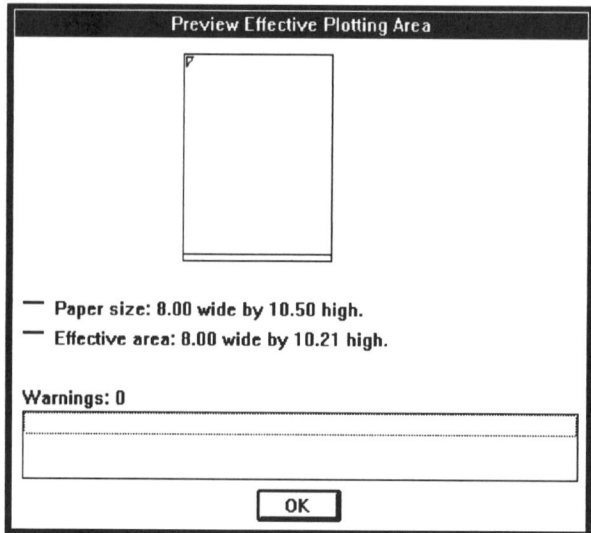

4. If the two rectangles don't mostly overlap, you need to rotate the plot by 90 degrees. Click on **OK** to exit plot preview, then click on **Rotation and Origin**. When the Plot Rotation and Origin dialog box appears, click on the radio button next to **90**, then click on **OK**. Recheck with the plot preview feature.

5. When the Plot Configuration dialog box reappears, click on the **OK** button. AutoCAD calculates the area that the drawing takes up on the paper and asks you to check that the printer has paper. When you are ready, press **Enter** to begin the plot.
   Effective plotting area: 8.00 wide by 10.21 high
   Position paper in printer.
   Press RETURN to continue or S to Stop for hardware setup: **[Enter]**

6. As AutoCAD sends the drawing data to the printer, it reports on the time to regenerate the drawing data.
   Regeneration done 100%
   Sending to System Printer.
   Plot Complete.
   Command:

AutoCAD converts its vector drawing into the raster format required by the LaserJet printer. If you find the plot takes too long, set the LaserJet for a lower resolution, such as 150dpi in the Windows Control Panel.

Congratulations! You've drafted your very first drawing using a computer. You can date the drawing and save it as a memento of your introduction to computer-aided drafting.

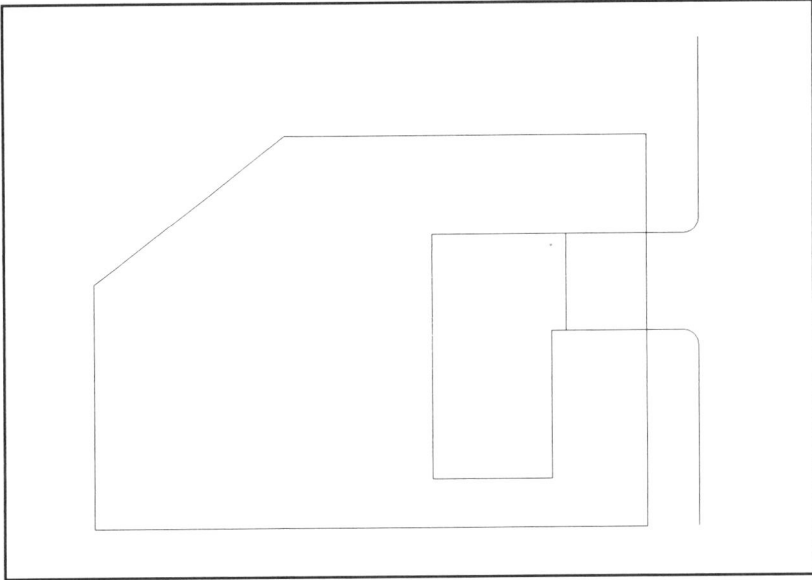

In the next chapter, you learn how AutoCAD makes repetitive drafting a snap. You also learn how to draw arcs and circles and add hatching to the drawing.

Hour 3

ADDING DETAILS TO THE LANDSCAPE PLAN

INTRODUCTION

In the last hour, you created the outlines of the lot, the house and the roadways. This hour, you add details to the yard, such as the lawn, trees, and a pool.

DIVIDING THE LOT

The yard has a lawn and a garden area. You draw the boundary between the two areas with a polyline, then smooth it with the PEdit command.

1. Before starting the PLine command, make sure the working layer is set to **Lawn**. Select layer Lawn from the toolbar.
2. Select **Draw|Polyline** from the menu bar.
   Command: _pline
   From point:

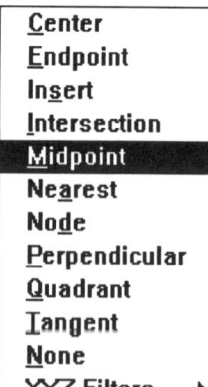

3. Hold down the **Shift** key on the keyboard, press the rightmost mouse button, then let go of the Shift key. A new menu pops up on the screen. This menu lists all AutoCAD's object snap modes. Click **Midpoint**.

40

4. Move the cursor to anywhere on the diagonal lot line and pick it.
   From point: _mid of **[pick diagonal lot line]**

AutoCAD snaps the beginning of the polyline to the exact midpoint of the diagonal line.

5. Pick a few more points at roughly 10' to 20' intervals, moving your way down to the bottom yard line.

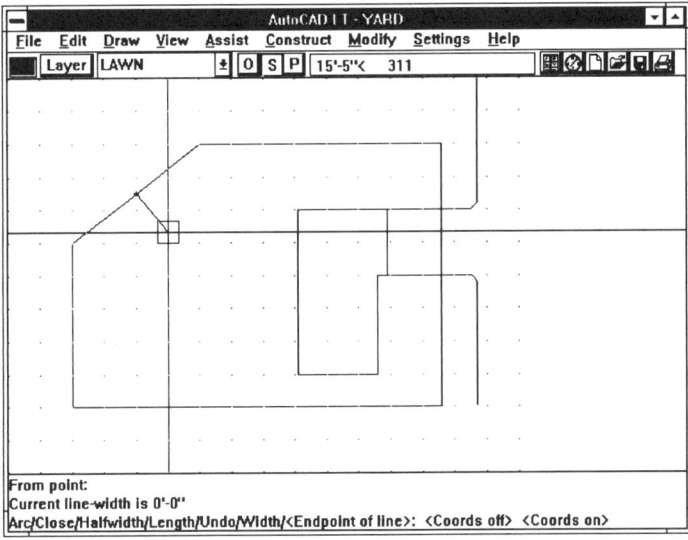

If you cannot tell how far 10 feet is, move the cursor to the coordinate display and click on it twice or until you see the display change to relative coordinates, similar to 15'-5"< 311, which means the cursor is currently 15'5" from the last picked point, at an angle of 311 degrees (measured counterclockwise from east).

6. When you get to the bottom lot line, press **Shift+right mouse button** and select **Midpoint** again. Pick any point where the line crosses the cursor's aperture box. Once again, AutoCAD snaps the polyline to the precise midpoint of the lot line.

7. Press **Ctrl+C** to end the PLine command.

41

SMOOTHING THE POLYLINE (Modify|Edit Polyline)

Here is the reason you created the boundary as a polyline: you now use the PEdit (short for polyline edit) command to smooth the straight polyline segments into a flowing curve. If you had used the Line command, you couldn't smooth the lines.

1. To edit the polyline, begin the PEdit command by selecting **Modify|Edit Polyline** from the menu. AutoCAD responds as follows:

   Command: _pedit
   Select polyline: **[pick polyline]**

2. Pick the polyline.

3. The PEdit command has many options. Its purpose is to let you change the look of a polyline. You use the Spline curve option to smooth the straight lines into a flowing curve, as follows:

   Close/Join/Width/Edit vertex/Fit/Spline/Decurve/Ltype gen/
   Undo/eXit <X>: **s**

The straight lines disappear and are replaced by a smooth curve. (Technically, AutoCAD redrew the line segments as a cubic Bezier curve based on the polyline frame.)

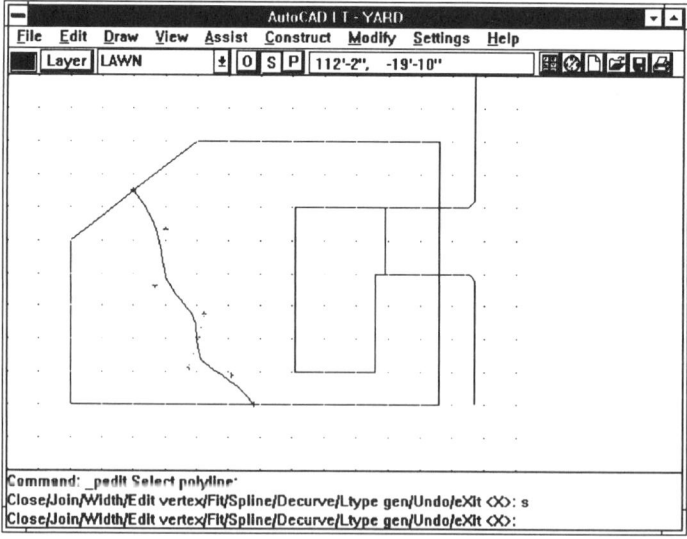

4. To exit the PEdit command, just type x, as follows:
   Close/.../eXit <X>: **x**
   Command:

The default is the X option, short for exit.

NON-MODAL EDITING

Earlier we began the PEdit command, then selected the polyline to edit. This is called "verb-noun" editing or "modal" editing. The verb is the command (PEdit); the noun is the object (the polyline). Model editing means that you first go into a mode (the PEdit command mode) before performing the action, selecting the polyline and the editing option.

In AutoCAD LT, you have the option to first pick the object, then move or stretch it into place. This is called "noun-verb" editing or "non-modal" editing. Non-modal editing is a faster way to edit. Here we use non-model editing to change the shape of the splined polyline separating the garden from the lawn.

1. Use Zoom command to enlarge the view of the splined polyline. Select **View|Zoom|Window** from the menu bar. AutoCAD automatically supplies the W option to the Zoom command.
   Command: '_zoom
   All/.../Window/<Scale(X/XP)>: _window
   First corner:

2. The Window option of the Zoom command lets you specify the rectangular area on the screen you want magnified. When you pick two "corners," you specify the two opposite corners of the rectangle (see following figure).

Hour 3

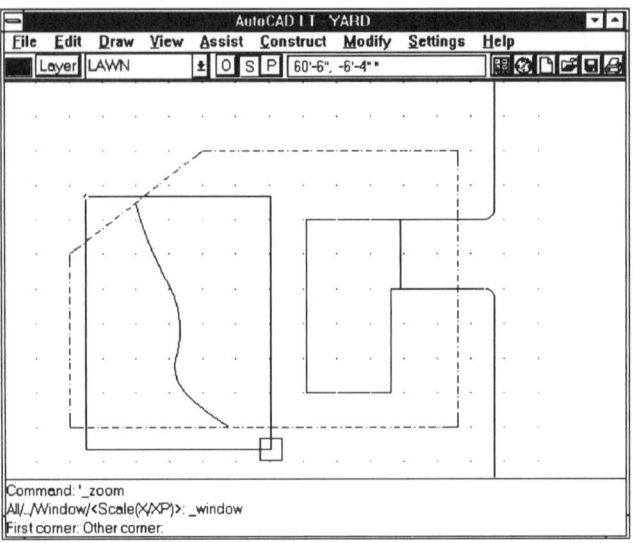

All/.../Window/<Scale(X/XP)>: _window
First corner: **[pick]**
Other corner: **[pick]**

3. In Hour 1, we pointed out the small square at the center of the crosshair cursor. We called it the "pickbox." When AutoCAD displays the pickbox, you are allowed to pick an object without first starting an editing command.

Pick the polyline. Notice that a number of blue squares appear on either side of the polyline, including one at both ends. The blue squares are called "grips," since they let you grip objects.

Adding Details to the Landscape Plan

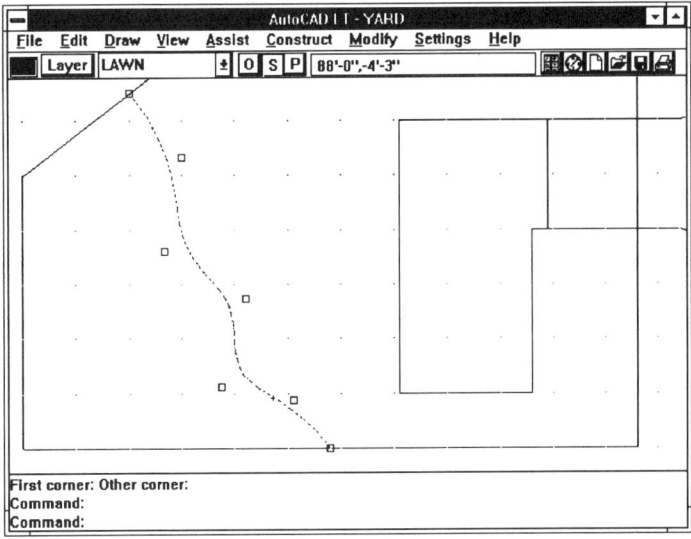

4. Now pick the blue square at the bottom end of the polyline. It turns solid red and the polyline changes from solid to dashed. The red square is known as a "hot" grip since editing commands affect it and not the "cold" blue squares.

5. In addition to the solitary red square, a prompt appears in the command area:

   ** STRETCH **
   <Stretch to point>/Base point/Copy/Undo/eXit: **nea**
   to **[pick lot line]**

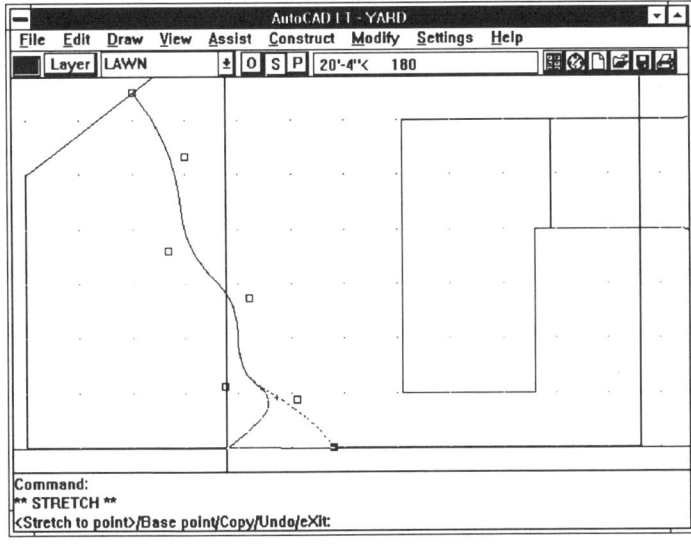

Hour 3

As you move the cursor, the last segment of the polyline curves and arcs to follow you. Click along the lot line where you want the end of the polyline to move. The NEAr object snap ensures the polyline ends precisely at the lot line.

6. You can interactively reshape the entire polyline, segment by segment. The grips indicate the vertices of the straight polyline segments you originally drew before splining with PEdit.
7. When you are finished reshaping the polyline, press **Ctrl+C** twice to exit modeless editing.
8. Use the **View|Zoom|All** command to see the entire drawing again.

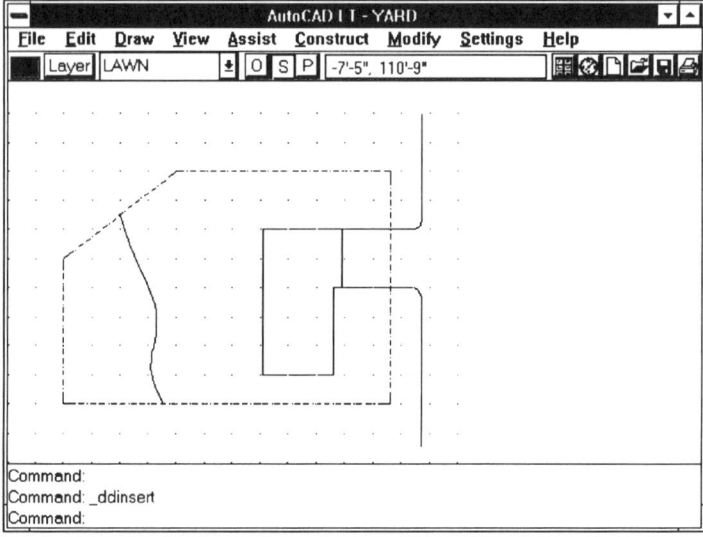

CREATING THE HATCH BOUNDARY

You have created the boundary between lawn and garden, but how do you tell the difference? One way is to add a grass symbol to the lawn area. In AutoCAD LT, this is done with the Hatch command. You apply a hatch pattern to a drawing in two steps: (1) draw a hatch perimeter; (2) apply the hatch pattern inside the perimeter.

The hatch perimeter contains the pattern. You use the lawn/garden boundary as part of the hatch perimeter, but you need to enclose the

Adding Details to the Landscape Plan

entire area. Otherwise, the pattern "leaks" out and covers the entire drawing.

1. Create a new layer to hold the hatch boundary, as follows:

   Command: **layer**
   ?/Make/.../Unlock: **m**
   New layer name: **hatch**
   ?/Make/.../Unlock: **[Enter]**

The Make option creates the new Hatch layer and sets it as the current working layer, all in a single command.

2. With the Hatch layer created, let's create the hatch boundary as a polyline. Select **Draw|Polyline**.
3. When AutoCAD prompts you to pick the from-point, respond by selecting **Assist|Object Snap** from the menu bar. AutoCAD displays the Running Object Snap dialog box.

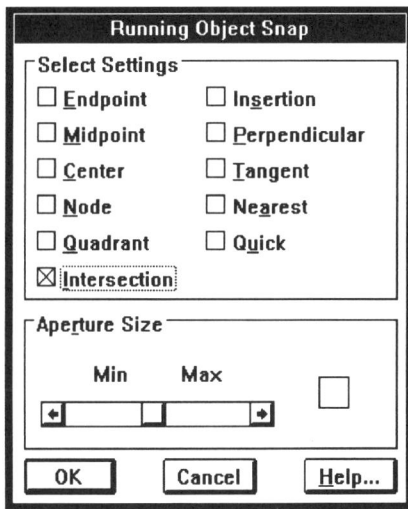

Previously, you pressed Shift+right mouse button to temporarily set an object snap mode. This new dialog box lists the names of all AutoCAD object snap modes and lets you interactively change the size of the aperture around the crosshair cursor. In addition, it keeps the object snap mode turned on until you explicitly turn the mode off.

4. Click on **Endpoint** and on the **OK** button. The dialog box disappears and the PLine command continues. Take a look at the command prompt area, which should appear as follows:

47

```
Command: _pline
From point: '_ddosnap
From point:
```

When you selected Draw|Polyline from the menu bar, AutoCAD executed the PLine command. The underscore (_) in front of "_pline" ensures the command works, no matter which language of AutoCAD is in use. (AutoCAD is available in a dozen different languages.)

When you selected Assist|Object Snap from the menu bar, AutoCAD executed the DdOsnap command, which displays the Running Object Snap dialog box. The prefix "Dd" indicates that this command displays a dialog box.

The apostrophe (') in front of '_ddosnap indicates the command is "transparent." A transparent command is used during another command and on its own at the Command: prompt. The following is Autodesk's list of transparent commands in AutoCAD LT:

'About	'DdUnits	'QText
'AttDisp	'Dist	'Redraw
'Base	'Fill	'Script
'DdEmodes	'Help	'Style
'DdGrips	'Id	'Tilemode
'DdLmodes	'Limits	'Time
'DdOsnap	'Linetype	'Unlock
'DdPtype	'Ltscale	'View
'DdRmodes	'Osnap	'Zoom
'Ddselect	'Pan	

The majority of AutoCAD commands are not transparent.

5. Now complete drawing the polyline, picking the points shown in the figure.

Adding Details to the Landscape Plan

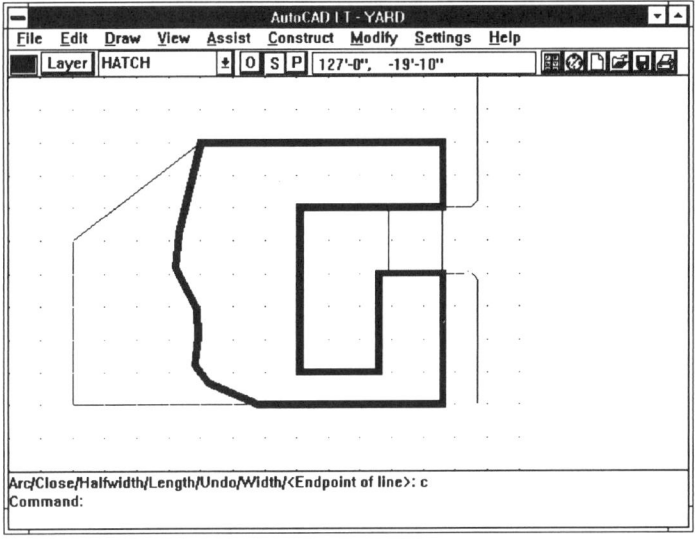

HATCHING THE LAWN (Draw|Hatch)

With the hatch boundary in place, you now use the Hatch command to apply the grass hatch pattern.

1. First, switch back to the Lawn layer via the toolbar.
2. Select **Draw|Hatch** to start the Hatch command and AutoCAD displays the Select Hatch Pattern icon menu:

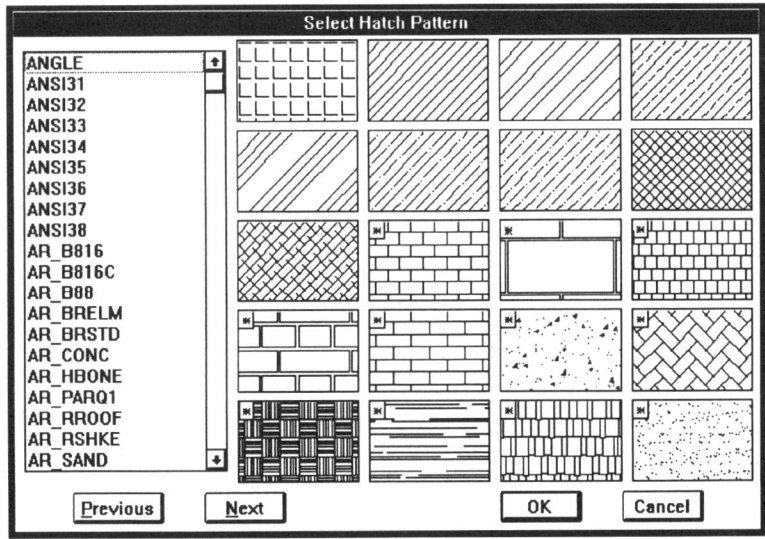

49

3. Since we don't see the grass hatch pattern, click on the **Next** button.
4. There it is! Click on the grass hatch pattern or on the word "GRASS" in the list of names.
5. Click on the **OK** button and AutoCAD prompts you for information related to the Hatch command, as follows:

   Command: _hatch
   Pattern (? or name/U,style)<u>: grass
   Scale for pattern <1.0000>: **50**

First, you need to decide on the scale factor. Use a large scale factor, such as 50, to make the pattern visible. Type 50 and press Enter.

6. AutoCAD asks for the angle of the hatch pattern, as follows:

   Angle for pattern <0>: **[Enter]**

Accept the default value of zero degrees (shown in the angle brackets) by pressing the Enter key.

7. Now, AutoCAD asks what to hatch. Pick the bounding polyline you created earlier, as follows.

   Select objects: **[pick hatch boundary polyline]**
   Select objects: **[Enter]**

After you press Enter, AutoCAD quickly hatches the lawn area. Note how precisely AutoCAD applied the hatch pattern, and how it automatically clips the pattern along boundaries. Try doing a hatch pattern that neatly and that quickly by hand!

With all this hard work on your drawing, it's a good idea to save the drawing to the computer's hard disk with the Save command... right now!

CREATING A SYMBOL (Draw|Circle, Construct|Array)

Let's add some trees and shrubs to the garden area. You draw the symbol for a tree out of a circle and an array of lines. After you draw one tree symbol, you add several more with a single command.

1. Before starting the first tree, make sure the working layer is set to Plants (select layer Plants from the toolbar).
2. Select **Draw|Circle|Center,Radius** to draw a six-inch radius circle, as follows:

Adding Details to the Landscape Plan

```
Command: _circle
3P/TTR/<Center point>: [pick in garden area]
Radius: 6
```

AutoCAD LT has three ways to draw a circle. Here you have used the most common method: pick the circle's center point and specify the radius of the circle. When you specify a radius of 6, AutoCAD draws a circle with a 1-foot diameter.

3. The 1-foot circle looks very small on the screen. The Zoom command lets you see your work more clearly. Select **View|Zoom|Window**. (As an alternative, click on the magnifying lens button on the toolbar, if visible.)

```
Command: _zoom
All/Center/Dynamic/Extents/Previous/Window/<Scale(X/XP)>:
    _window
First corner: [pick point]
Other corner: [pick point]
```

Pick the points on diagonal corners either side of the circle. If the circle doesn't look large enough, repeat the Zoom Window command.

4. Oops! What happened to the circle? If the circle looks like an octagon on your screen, select **View|Regen** to clean it up, as follows:

```
Command: _regen
Regenerating drawing.
```

5. Now that the circle looks rounder and larger, it is easier to work with. To draw the array of lines (representing the branches), you draw one line and then use the Array command to create the array. Select **Draw|Line**, as follows:

```
Command: _line
From point: cen
of [pick circle]
To point: [pick point anywhere outside of circle]
To point: [Enter]
```

Here you used the CENter object snap to begin the line at the precise center of the circle. The other end of the line goes just beyond the edge of the circle.

51

Hour 3

6. Repeat the branch line 24 times with the Array command. Select **Construct|Array** from the menu, as follows:

   Command: _array
   Select objects: **L**
   1 found Select objects: **[Enter]**
   Rectangular or Polar array (R/P) <R>: **p**
   Center point of array: **cen**
   of **[pick circle]**
   Number of items: **25**
   Angle to fill (+=ccw,-=cw) <360>: **[Enter]**
   Rotate objects as they are copied? [Y> **[Enter]**

AutoCAD quickly draws 24 more lines around the circle, completing the tree symbol.

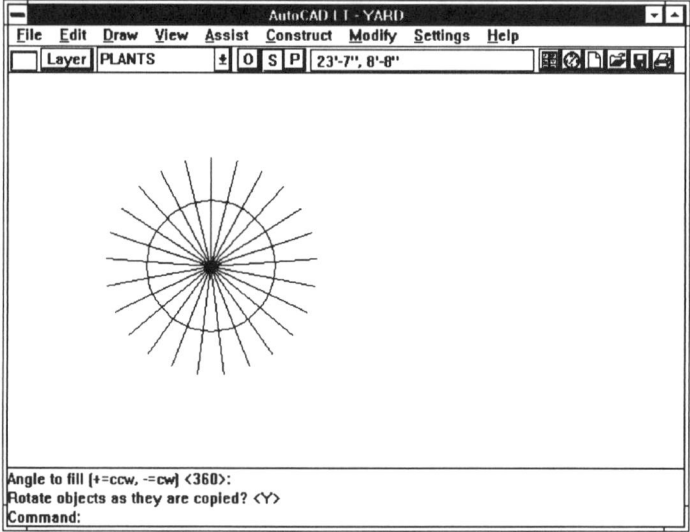

When the Array command asks you to select the objects to array, you can respond with the letter "L" (short for Last). This is AutoCAD's shorthand notation for selecting the last object drawn *still visible on the screen.* "L" works as a response whenever a command prompts you with "Select objects:".

You typed in "p" for polar array; the Array command also creates a rectangular array of objects. The Array command has a quirk: if you want to array an object 24 times, you have to specify 25 as the number of items. AutoCAD considers the original item as the first arrayed item.

Adding Details to the Landscape Plan

You can simply press the Enter key for the last two questions. Pressing Enter is AutoCAD's shorthand to accept the default value shown in the angle brackets, such as <360> degrees.

MAKING A SYMBOL (Construct|Make Block)

Although CAD lets you draw a symbol, such as the tree symbol, fairly quickly, there are many keystrokes involved. You reduce the keystrokes by turning the symbol into a "block" and then inserting the block into the drawing. Here you add several more trees to the garden area.

1. To turn the tree symbol into a block, use AutoCAD LT's BMake command (short for "block make"). Select **Construct|Make Block** from the menu bar and AutoCAD displays the Block Definition dialog box.

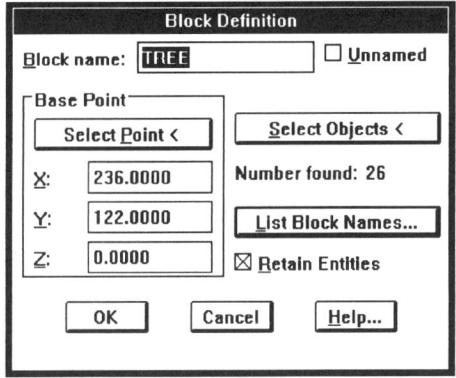

2. Type **tree** in the text entry box next to Block name. You can give the block any name you like up to 31 characters long; for practical purposes, you should keep the name under nine characters.

3. The "base point" is used later by the Insert command as the point where the block is placed in the drawing. The center of the tree symbol is a logical insertion point; using the CENter object snap ensures a precise pick. Click on the **Select Point** button. The dialog box disappears and AutoCAD prompts:

   Insertion base point: **cen**
   of **[pick circle]**

53

The dialog box reappears with the x, y, z coordinates of the base point filled in.

4. Finally, you need to tell AutoCAD which objects to turn into a block. AutoCAD lets you select objects several different ways. So far, you have picked them (one at a time) with your mouse or with the "L" option. Just as you windowed the zoomed-in view, you can window the objects you want to select with the "w" option (short for window). Click on the **Select Objects** button. The dialog box disappears and AutoCAD prompts:

   Select objects: **w**
   First corner: **[pick corner]**
   Other corner: **[pick corner]**
   26 found Select objects: **[Enter]**

You pick the two corners of a rectangle that encompasses the circle and 25 lines making up the tree symbol. Make sure that all 26 objects are inside the selection rectangle; otherwise AutoCAD won't include them. The dialog box reappears and reports "Number found: 26."

5. Click on the **OK** button and AutoCAD removes the dialog box and records the tree symbol as a block.

ADDING MANY MORE TREES
(Aerial View, Draw|Insert Block)

Now that the tree symbol is a block, you insert it into the drawing. First, though, we need to see more of the garden area. We could use the Zoom command to enlarge the view. However, AutoCAD LT includes a handy drawing viewer, named Aerial View, that lets you easily zoom and pan about the drawing.

1. First, click on the compass icon on the toolbar (second icon button from the left).

   Or, select **Settings|Aerial View** from the menu bar.

   Or, type DsViewer at the Command prompt, as follows:
   Command: **dsviewer**

Adding Details to the Landscape Plan

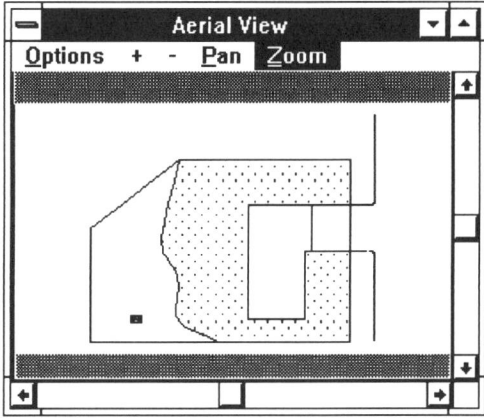

Any of these three actions causes AutoCAD to launch the Aerial View window. Like the toolbox, Aerial View is an independent window that floats anywhere on the Windows desktop. It always shows you the full extent of the drawing, no matter how far in or out you zoom. If you look closely, you see a small black square where you drew the tree: that is Aerial View's way of showing where AutoCAD's current zoomed-in view is located.

2. The word "Zoom" is highlighted on the Aerial View's menu bar. That means that zoom is the default mode. Zoom out from the tree by clicking two points on the Aerial View window, as shown in the figure below.

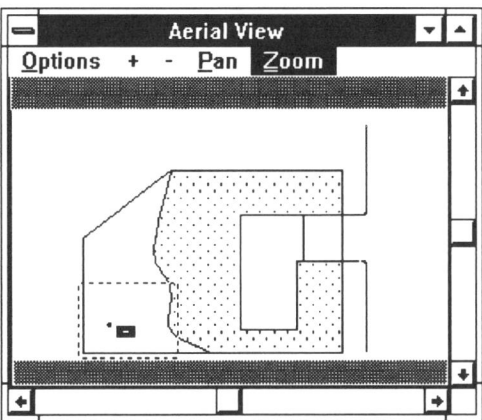

AutoCAD immediately zooms out and a new, larger rectangle shows the new view in the Aerial View window.

55

Hour 3

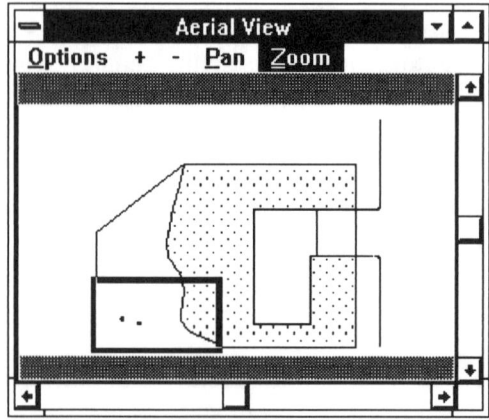

(If you find Aerial View too frustrating, do a Zoom All followed by a Zoom Window, as follows:

Command: **zoom**
All/.../ Window/<Scale(X/XP)>: **a**
Regenerating drawing.
Command: **[Enter]**
All/.../ Window/<Scale(X/XP)>: **w**
First corner: **[pick]**
Other corner: **[pick]**

5. Now place a 5'-tree symbol by selecting **Draw|Insert Block** from the menu bar. AutoCAD displays the Insert dialog box.

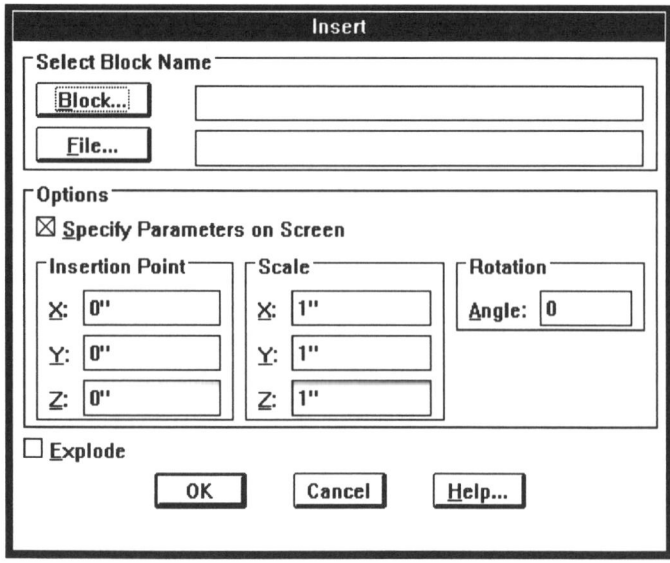

Adding Details to the Landscape Plan

6. Since the only block you've defined in this drawing is Tree, AutoCAD automatically lists the name. You can ignore everything else in the dialog box and click on the **OK** button.

(If you find the Aerial View window getting in the way, simply slide it off the side of the screen or type the undocumented DsViewer_Off command to remove it entirely.)

7. AutoCAD prompts you for the following information:
   Block name (or ?): **tree**
   Insertion point: **[pick a point in the garden area]**

8. When you supply an X-scale factor, AutoCAD draws the block larger or smaller than the original symbol.
   X scale factor <1> / Corner / XYZ: **5**

When you specify an X-scale factor of 5, AutoCAD draws the block five times larger. Since you drew the original symbol 1 foot in diameter, the newly inserted tree is 5 feet in diameter. You can see that it makes sense to draw a symbol to unit size (to the nearest inch or foot) that makes it easy to scale the block during insertion.

9. If you want to stretch or squeeze the block, the Insert command allows you to specify a different Y-scale factor. This is useful for inserting rectangles (such as different sized lumber) based on a unit square.
   Y scale factor (default=X): **[Enter]**

10. You insert blocks at an angle by responding to the "Rotation angle" prompt with an angle. Since the tree symbol is round, it makes no sense to insert it at an angle.
    Rotation angle <0.0000>: **[Enter]**

11. Add several more trees around the garden area using the Insert command and different X-scale factors, such as 6.0, 4.0, 2.0, and 1.5 (see following figure).

57

Hour 3

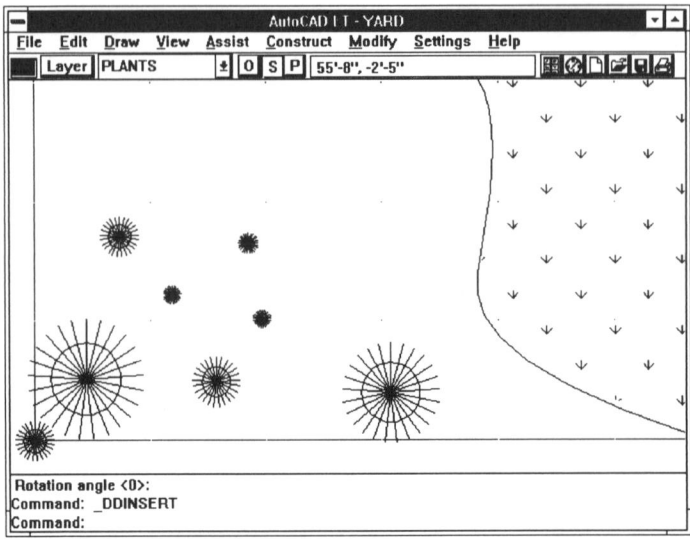

12. Anytime you want to see the list of blocks defined in the current drawing, select **Construct|Make Block** and click on the **List Block Names** button. AutoCAD displays another dialog box with a list of block names that currently exist in the drawing.

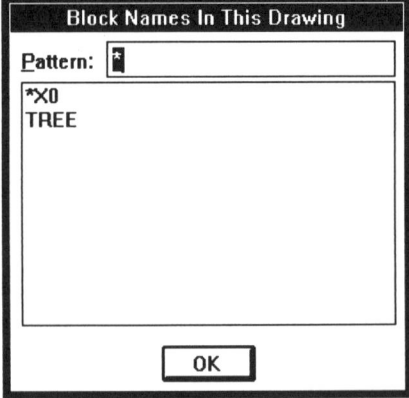

The Block Names in this Drawing dialog box lists the name of the Tree block you created plus another block named *X0, which is the grass hatch pattern. AutoCAD stores hatch patterns (and associative dimensions) as blocks in the drawing. Click on the two **Cancel** buttons to dismiss the dialog boxes.

DRAWING THE POND
(Pan, Draw|Ellipse, Construct|Offset)

Drawing the garden pond illustrates another pair of AutoCAD commands. You draw the oval-shaped pond with the Ellipse command and add the pond's edging with the Offset command.

1. Switch to the Pond layer via the toolbar.
2. If you need more space to draw in, use Aerial View to pan the view upwards. First, select **Pan** from the Aerial View's menu bar. Next, move the mouse so that the dotted rectangle moves up. Finally, click the mouse's leftmost button to reposition the view in AutoCAD.

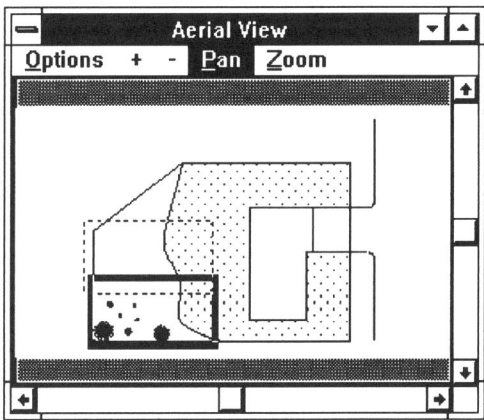

3. The pond is an oval 15 feet long and 5 feet wide. Draw the pond with the Ellipse command. Select **Draw|Ellipse** from the menu.
   Command: _ellipse
   <Axis endpoint 1>/Center: **[pick]**

Pick the starting point of the ellipse anywhere in the garden area.

4. The other end of the pond is 15 feet away, with the pond angling at 300 degrees.
   Axis endpoint 2: **@15'<300**

5. And the pond is 5 feet wide:
   <Other axis distance>/Rotation: **5'**

6. You could draw the rock edging of the pond by reusing the Ellipse command, but it probably wouldn't be precisely centered.

Instead, the Offset command creates a concentric ellipse. Select **Construct|Offset** from the menu bar, as follows:

Command: _offset
Offset distance or Through <Through>: **1'**
Select object to offset: **[pick ellipse]**
Side to offset? **[pick outside ellipse]**
Select object to offset: **[Enter]**

The Offset command also creates parallel lines, parallel polylines, and concentric circles and arcs.

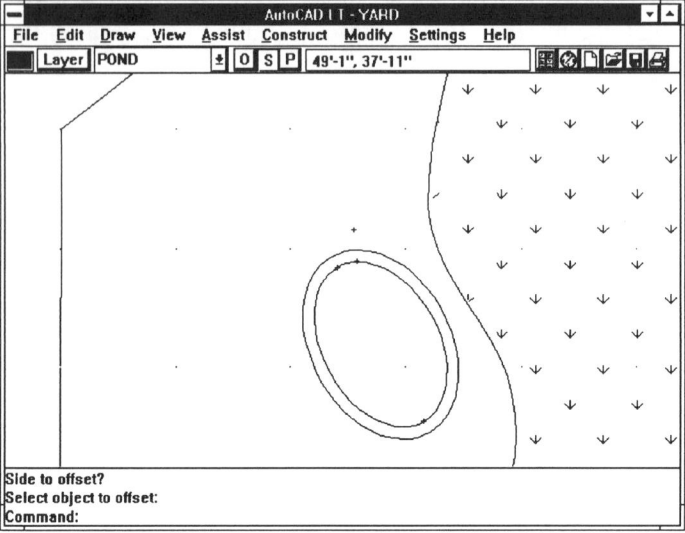

Remember to save your work with the Save command. To see the progress you are making in learning AutoCAD, plot your drawing with the Plot command by clicking on the printer icon on the toolbar.

Adding Details to the Landscape Plan

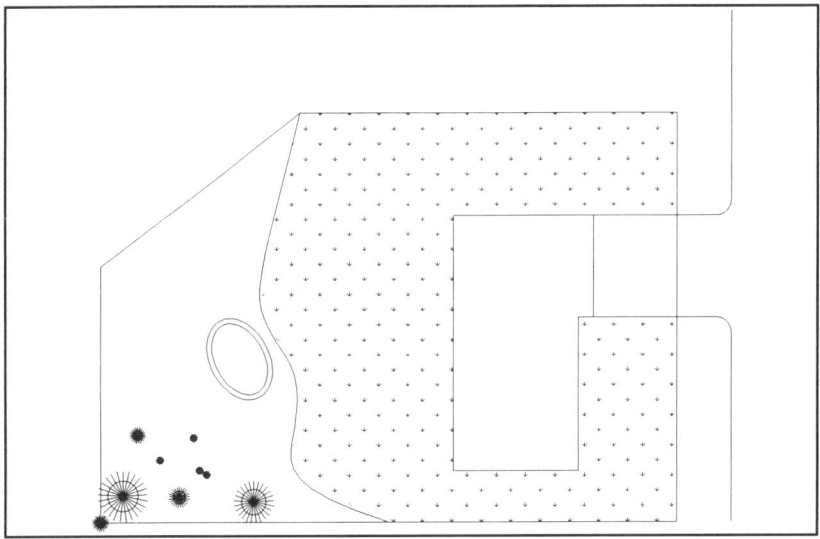

In this hour, you added details to the landscape plan. With drawing commands such as Hatch, Circle, Block, and Ellipse you drafted the lawn, trees, and pond. Editing commands such as PEdit, Array, Insert, and Offset made the tedious job of drawing details much faster. Finally, you saw how the Aerial View window makes it easier to move around the drawing.

Next hour, you learn some of AutoCAD's inquiry commands to get information out of the drawing. You also add a fence, change colors of objects, and modify the shape of the pond.

Hour 4
CHANGING THE LANDSCAPE

INTRODUCTION

In the last hour, you added details to the drawing, such as the lawn, some trees, and a pond. This hour you learn how to change parts of the yard and how to get information out of the drawing.

CHANGING THE LOOK OF LINES
(Settings|Linetype, Modify|Change Properties, LtScale)

When you drew the lot lines in the second hour, they showed up on the screen as a solid line. However, lot lines are usually shown in a dashed pattern. Just as AutoCAD comes with several hatching patterns, it also includes eight line patterns, called "linetypes."

To change from a solid line (called "continuous" by AutoCAD) to a dashed linetype takes two steps: (1) load the linetype; and (2) change the line to the new linetype.

1. First, do a Zoom All so that you see the entire drawing on the screen, as follows:
   Command: **zoom**
   All/.../<Scale (X/XP)>: **a**
   Regenerating drawing.

2. The linetype definitions are stored in a separate definition file (called aclt.lin) on the hard drive. Before you can use a linetype,

you have to load it into the drawing. Select **Settings|Linetype Style|Load**.

3. AutoCAD prompts you which linetypes to load, as follows:
   ```
   Command: '_linetype
   ?/Create/Load/Set: _load
   Linetype(s) to load: *
   ```

When you type "*" (shorthand for load *all* linetype definitions), AutoCAD pops up a dialog box. Pick the **OK** button.

4. AutoCAD then lists the linetype names as it loads them:
   ```
   Linetype BORDER loaded.
   Linetype BORDER2 loaded.
   Linetype BORDERX2 loaded.
   Linetype CENTER loaded.
   Linetype CENTER2 loaded.
   Linetype CENTERX2 loaded.
   Linetype DASHDOT loaded.
   Linetype DASHDOT2 loaded.
   Linetype DASHDOTX2 loaded.
   Linetype DASHED loaded.
   Linetype DASHED2 loaded.
   Linetype DASHEDX2 loaded.
   Linetype DIVIDE loaded.
   Linetype DIVIDE2 loaded.
   Linetype DIVIDEX2 loaded.
   Linetype DOT loaded.
   Linetype DOT2 loaded.
   Linetype DOTX2 loaded.
   Linetype HIDDEN loaded.
   Linetype HIDDEN2 loaded.
   Linetype HIDDENX2 loaded.
   Linetype PHANTOM loaded.
   Linetype PHANTOM2 loaded.
   Linetype PHANTOMX2 loaded.
   ?/Create/Load/Set: [Enter]
   ```

Press **F2** to view the linetype names; press **F2** again to flip back to your drawing screen.

I find it easier to load all linetypes at once, rather than loading the one that you currently need. That saves you from going through the load procedure each time you need another linetype.

Hour 4

4. The ChProp (short for change properties) command changes a number of attributes of an object, including changing linetypes. You use it here to change the lot lines from continuous to border. Select **Modify|Change Property** from the menu bar.

5. AutoCAD prompts you to select the lot lines, as follows:

   Command: _ddchprop
   Select objects: **[pick first line]**
   1 selected, 1 found Select objects: **[pick second line]**
   1 selected, 1 found Select objects: **[pick third line]**
   1 selected, 1 found Select objects: **[pick fourth line]**
   1 selected, 1 found Select objects: **[pick fifth line]**
   1 selected, 1 found Select objects: **[Enter]**

6. After you finish selecting lines, AutoCAD displays the Change Properties dialog box. This dialog box lets you change the color, layer, linetype, and thickness of the selected entities.

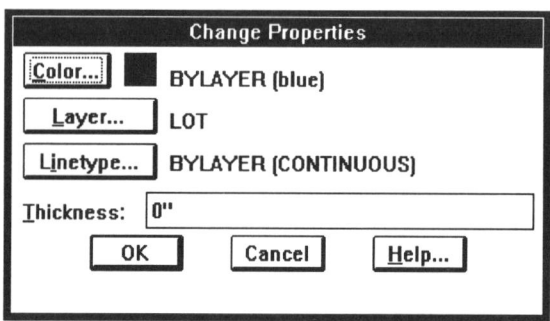

Click on the **Linetype** button and AutoCAD displays the Select Linetype dialog box.

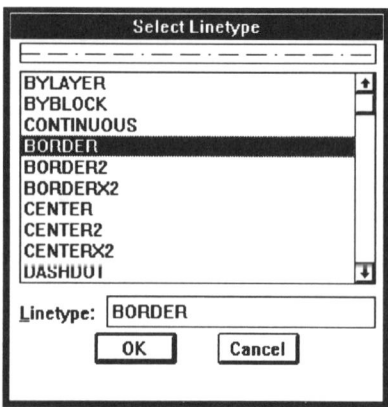

7. Select the Border linetype by clicking on **BORDER**, then clicking on the **OK** button.
8. Click on the **OK** button to exit the Change Properties dialog box.
9. You see the lot lines redraw on the screen and yet look solid. That's because the dash-dot pattern is being drawn at a very small scale. You enlarge the linetype scale with the LtScale command. Select **Settings|Linetype Style|Linetype Scale**. AutoCAD prompts you, as follows:

   Command: _ltscale
   New scale factor <1.0000>: **50**
   Regenerating drawing.

Type the same scale factor as you used for the hatch pattern, 50. AutoCAD now redraws the lot lines with the border linetype visible. That process was a lot easier than using an eraser shield!

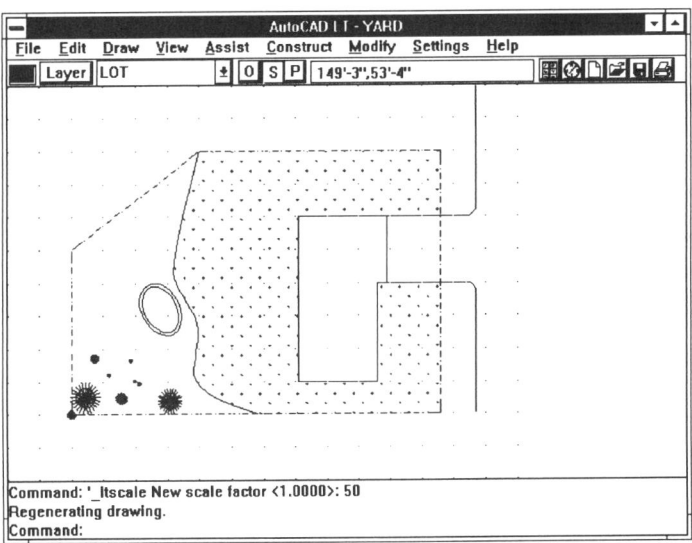

CHANGING LINE LENGTHS (Modify|Change Points)

As an example of how the Change command changes the size of an entity, extend the edge of the street to the bottom of the screen, as follows:

1. Before starting the Change command, click on the toolbar's "O" button to turn on ortho mode. This ensures the changes are made perfectly vertical.
2. Select **Modify|Change Points** from the menu bar.
3. Pick the road line, as follows:
   Command: <Ortho on> _change
   Select objects: **[pick road line]**
   1 selected, 1 found
   Select objects: **[Enter]**
4. When prompted with <Change point>, pick a point at the bottom of the screen below the end of the road line. It doesn't matter if you are directly below the line.
   Properties/<Change point>: **[pick point]**

AutoCAD extends the line to the bottom of the screen.

5. Turn off ortho mode by clicking on the toolbar's "O" again.
   Command: <Ortho off>

CHANGING THE LOOK OF THE POND (Modify|Stretch)

So far, you have used several editing commands to change objects. You've used PEdit to modify polylines, non-model editing to stretch the sketch line, and the Change command to alter the appearance of lines.

One of AutoCAD's most powerful editing commands is called Stretch. The Stretch command lets you take part of an object and stretch it wider or thinner. Here you apply it to the pond to change its shape.

1. Select **Modify|Stretch** from the menu bar.
   Command: _stretch
   Select objects to stretch by window or polygon...
2. Despite the Stretch command's prompt to the contrary (it says "stretch by window"), crossing mode is the object selection mode you have to use the first time you select objects with the Stretch command, as follows.
   Select objects: **c**

"C" is short for "crossing," an object selection mode similar to the window mode you used with the Zoom command. In this case,

Changing the Landscape

AutoCAD selects all objects within the selection rectangle *and all objects crossing or touching the rectangle* (see following figure). You may find crossing mode somewhat faster than window mode since you don't have to draw as large a rectangle.

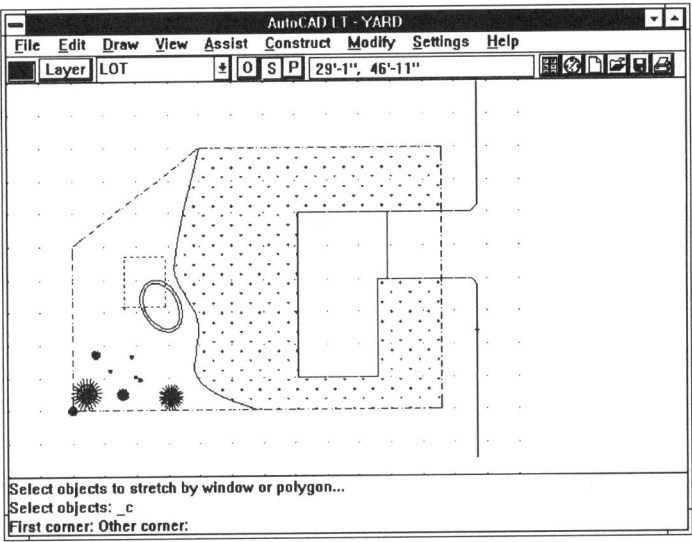

AutoCAD has 17 options for you to use during object selection, as shown in the following table. I find that I use only a few of the options, such as pick, W, C, L, P, and Enter.

Mode	Abbreviation	Meaning
Object	pick	Select a single object
Window	W	Select all objects within a rectangular window
Window Polygon	WP	Select all objects within a polygonal window
Crossing	C	Select object crossing and within a rectangular window
Crossing Polygon	CP	Select all objects crossing and within a polygon
Fence	F	Select objects along a fence polyline
Box	B	W or C mode, depends on cursor movement
Automatic	AU	Pick, W, or C mode, depending on pick point
Single	SI	Select first object encountered

Hour 4

Mode	Abbreviation	Meaning (Continued)
Last	L	Select most recently drawn object
Previous	P	Select most recently selected object
Multiple	M	Delay database scanning
Undo	U	Remove most recent selection group
Remove	R	Enter remove-objects mode
Add	A	Enter add-objects mode
End	Enter	End object selection
Cancel	Ctrl+C	Cancel object selection

   3. Pick two corners of a rectangle that covers part of the pond, as follows:

   First corner: **[pick]**
   Other corner: **[pick]**
   2 found Select objects: **[Enter]**

Notice how the crossing box is a dashed rectangle, which differs from the solid line used with the window box. If the pond were entirely inside the object selection rectangle, the Stretch command would only move the pond, not stretch it.

   4. To tell AutoCAD how much you want the pond stretched, pick two points that indicate the distance:

   Base point: **[pick near pond]**
   New point: **[pick away from pond]**

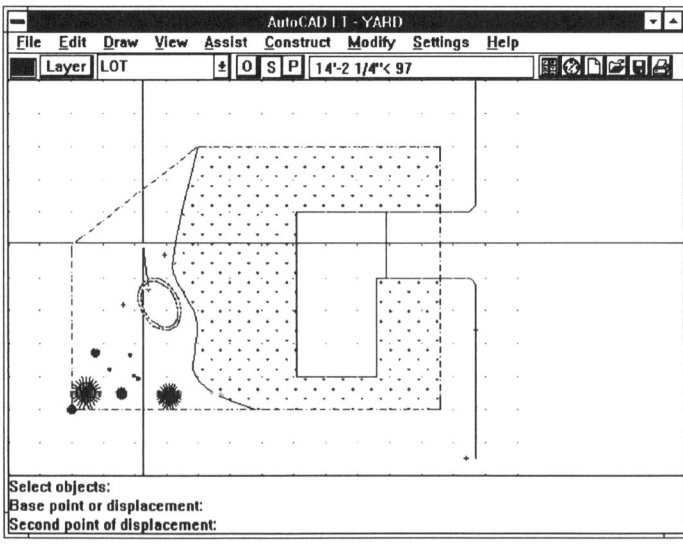

5. You have now created a whole new look to your pond! If you don't like it, you undo the stretch with the U command, as follows:

   Command: **u**
   U: STRETCH

   ... and try stretching the pond again.

6. If the pond isn't exactly where you want it, you relocate it with the Move command. Move the pond closer to the lawn, as follows:

   Command: **m**

Here you used another of AutoCAD's shortcuts. "M" is the abbreviation for the Move command. The complete list of command name abbreviations (called aliases) is in the file aclt.pgp. Some of the more common aliases are:

Alias	Command	Alias	Command
A	Arc	M	Move
B	Block	O	Osnap
C	Circle	P	Pan
CP	Copy	PL	Pline
D	Dim	R	Redraw
E	Erase	S	Stretch
F	Fillet	T	DText
G	Grid	V	View
H	Hatch	X	Explode
I	DdInsert	Z	Zoom
L	Line		

7. Continue the Move command, as follows:

   MOVE Select objects: **c**
   First corner: **[pick]**
   Other corner: **[pick]**
   1 found Select objects: **[Enter]**
   Base point or displacement: **[pick edge of pond]**
   Second point of displacement: **[pick new location]**

Hour 4

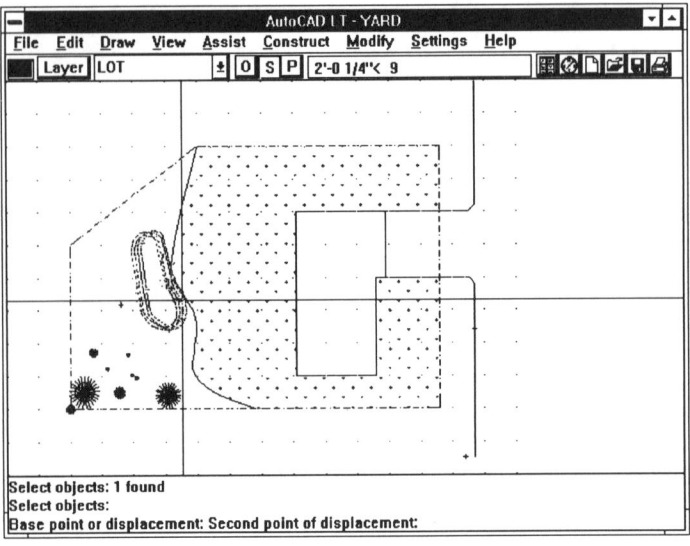

8. Clean up the screen with the Redraw command, as follows:
   Command: r
   REDRAW

MEASURING THE AREA OF THE LAWN (Assist|Area)

You've seen how to create a drawing in AutoCAD and how to change the drawing. AutoCAD is able to return to you in a useful form information stored in the drawing.

A common piece of information is the area of objects. If you need to know how much fertilizer to buy for your lawn, you use the Area command to find the lawn's area.

1. Thaw the Hatch layer to reuse the hatch outline:
   Command: **layer**
   ?/Make/.../Thaw/LOck/Unlock: **t**
   Thaw layer name: **hatch**
   ?/Make/.../Thaw/LOck/Unlock: **[Enter]**

Thawing a layer reverses the freezing action you performed earlier.

2. Select **Assist|Area** from the menu bar.
   Command: _area
   <First point>/Entity/Add/Subtract: **e**

Changing the Landscape

The Area command adds and subtracts areas. Its entity option finds the area of shapes, such as circles and polygons.

3. Pick the hatch outline:
   Select circle or polyline: **[pick hatch boundary]**
   Area = 628486.6 square in. (4364.490 square ft.),
   Perimeter = 380'-8 1/2"

Your answer varies depending on where you located the garden/lawn boundary. Now you know: you need fertilizer for about 4,400 square feet of lawn.

4. Since it is no longer needed, you freeze the Hatch layer:
   Command: **layer**
   ?/Make/.../Thaw/LOck/Unlock: **f**
   Layer(s) to freeze: **hatch**
   ?/Make/.../Thaw/LOck/Unlock: **[Enter]**

ADDING A FENCE (Assist|XYZ Filters, Assist|List, Assist|Dist)

You've decided to add a fence to the backyard. You can use AutoCAD to help you plan the materials you'll need. After you draw the fence as a polyline, you find out from AutoCAD how long that line is.

1. First, switch the working layer to House by selecting its name from the toolbar.
2. If you turned off the INTersection object snap, turn it back on with the **Assist|Object Snap** command.
3. The fence is drawn as a 4"-wide polyline. Along the way, you'll use a number of object snap modes and point filters. Begin the PLine command by selecting **Draw|Polyline**.
4. Start the polyline at the middle of the upper house line. Use the MIDdle object snap override to precisely locate the polyline's starting point, as follows:
   Command: _pline
   From point: **mid**
   of **[pick upper house line]**
   Current line-width is 0'-0"

71

Hour 4

5. To change the width of the polyline from zero to four inches, use the "w" option, as follows:

   Arc/Close/Halfwidth/Length/Undo/Width/<Endpoint of line>: **w**
   Starting width <0'-0">: **4"**
   Ending width <0'-4">: **[Enter]**

(You can specify a different starting and ending width to produce tapered polylines.)

6. Now that the starting point and width are set, continue drawing the fence. Follow the path shown by the arrowheads in the following figure.

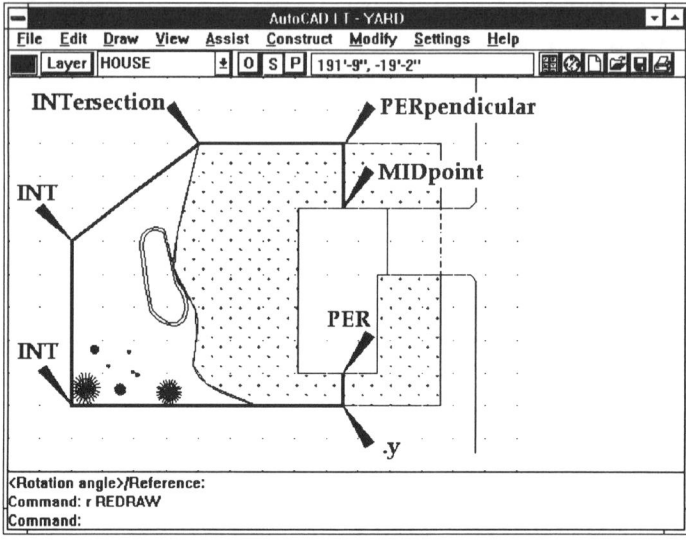

Arc/.../<Endpoint of line>: **per**
to **[pick upper lot line]**
Arc/.../<Endpoint of line>: **[pick upper right of diagonal]**
Arc/.../<Endpoint of line>: **[pick lower left of diagonal]**
Arc/.../<Endpoint of line>: **[pick lower left corner of lot]**

Pause the picking action here.

7. When you get to the bottom of the house, you get into a bit of tricky geometry. You want the fence to end at the same relative location as its starting point. Fortunately, AutoCAD finds that point for you through the use of "point filters."

Use the .y point filter on the bottom line of the lot, as follows:

Arc/.../<Endpoint of line>: **.y**
of **[pick lower left corner of lot line]**

Point filters let you enter a coordinate with a combination of screen pointing and keyboarding. When you use the ".y" point filter, you are telling AutoCAD that you want to pick the y-coordinate on the screen and will supply the x-coordinate from the keyboard. AutoCAD has six point filters, as shown in the following table:

Filter	*Picks*	*AutoCAD Needs*
.x	x	y- and z-coordinates
.y	y	x- and z-coordinates
.z	z	z- and y-coordinates
.xy	x and y	z-coordinate
.xz	x and z	y-coordinate
.yz	y and z	x-coordinate

As you can probably tell from the presence of the z-coordinate in the table, point filters are also used in three-dimensional drafting.

8. You're not sure of the x-coordinate, which is located somewhere along the bottom line of the lot. AutoCAD reminds you with the "(need X)" prompt, as follows:

   (need X): **mid**
   of **[pick upper house line]**

Pick the middle of the upper house line with the MIDdle object snap override.

9. Complete the fence by drawing the last polyline segment PERpendicular to the lower house line, as follows:

   Arc/.../<Endpoint of line>: **per**
   to **[pick lower house line]**
   Arc/.../<Endpoint of line>: **[Enter]**

10. Now that you've drawn the fence, use the List command to tell you the length. Select **Assist|List**.

    Command: **list**
    Select object: **[pick fence polyline]**
    1 selected 1 found
    Select objects: **[Enter]**

Hour 4

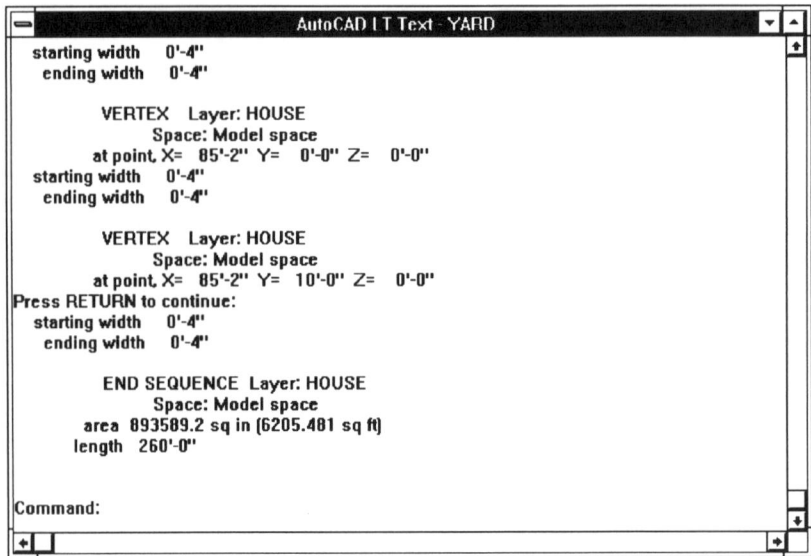

AutoCAD flips to the Text window and lists line after line of information. Whenever the listing pauses, press **Enter** until the Command: prompt reappears.

The List command is giving you every piece of information about the polyline that AutoCAD has stored in its database. Most of the information is about the vertices (the corners). The total length of the polyline is shown at the end of the listing: 260 feet. You now know how much fencing you need.

Press **F2** to flip back to the graphics window.

11. You can also measure distances directly on the drawing. The Dist command (short for distance) measures the distance between two points. Find the shortest distance from the house to the pond by selecting **Assist|Distance**, as follows:

Command: '_dist
First point: **nea**
to **[pick inside edge of pond]**
Second point: **per**
to **[pick house wall]**
Distance = 34'-5 1/2", Angle in X-Y Plane = 0, Angle from X-Y Plane = 0
Delta X = 34'-5 1/2", Delta Y = 0'-0", Delta Z = 0'-0"

The bee-line distance from house to pond is just over 34 feet. The value on your drawing may differ, depending on where you located the pond.

Remember to save the work you have done on the drawing. You may also want to plot out the drawing.

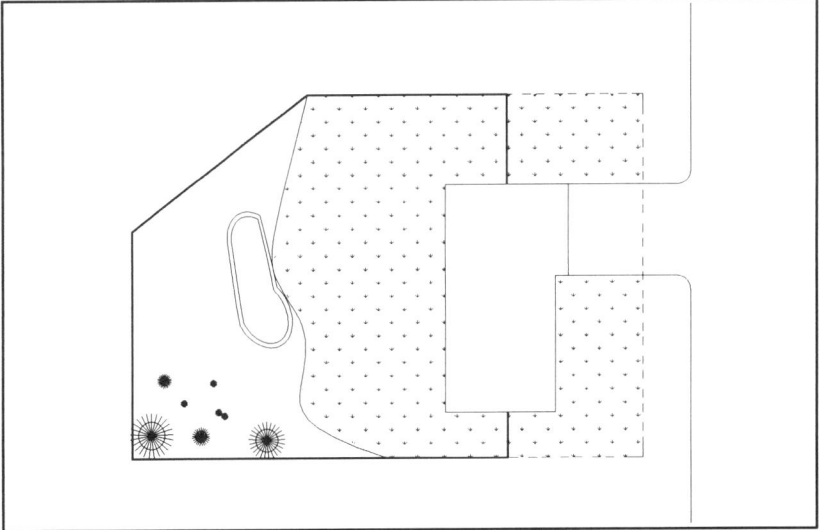

In this hour, you learned more about modifying the drawing with the Change and Stretch commands. You also learned about linetypes and how to calculate areas and find distances. Next hour, you learn how to add text, dimensions, and a title block to the drawing.

Hour 5

ADDING NOTES AND DIMENSIONS

INTRODUCTION

In the last hour, you changed parts of the yard and learned how to get some information out of the drawing. This hour, you add the finishing touches by drawing call-outs on the drawing and dimensioning the yard. You also learn how to save and restore named views of the drawing.

Bring the yard drawing into AutoCAD and do a Zoom All to make the full drawing visible. Make sure that the working layer is Text.

ADDING A NOTE TO THE DRAWING (Draw|Text)

With the yard plan largely complete, you now add call-outs to describe the different parts of the yard.

1. In AutoCAD LT, you add call-outs with the DText command (short for dynamic text). Select **Draw|Text** from the menu bar.
   Command: _dtext

2. Pick a starting point for the note within the house outline.
   Justify/Style/<Start point>: **[pick]**

3. The height of the text should be large enough to be legible when you plot the drawing. If you have been plotting the drawing on an A-size sheet of paper, you make an estimate of the drawing scale with the following calculation:

Adding Notes and Dimensions

> Height of drawing in real units: about 120'
> Width of A-size paper: about 8"
> Therefore, scale factor: about 120'*12/8" = 1:180

Now that you know the drawing scale, you determine how large to make the text with the following calculation:

> Height of plotted text: about 3/16"
> Height of text in real units: 3/16" * 180 = 34"

To get 3/16"-high text in the plotted output, you need to enter text 34" high on the AutoCAD drawing, as follows:

> Height <0'-3 1/2">: **34"**

If you have been plotting the drawing on larger paper, such as B-size, the text should be half as large, or 17".

4. Press Enter for the rotation angle since you want horizontal text, as follows:

    Rotation angle <0.0000>: **[Enter]**

5. Type the label "House" and press Enter; AutoCAD immediately draws the word House.

    Text: **House**

6. Press Enter to exit the DText command.

    Text: **[Enter]**

7. Zoom in on the word "House" to get a closer look at it, as follows:

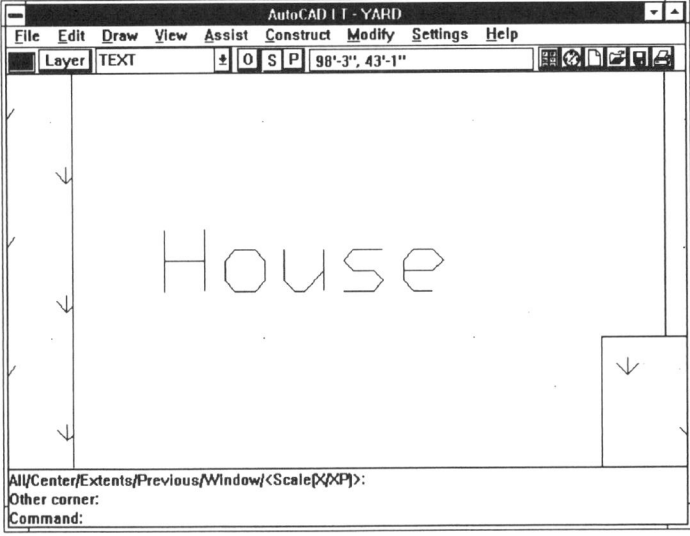

77

Hour 5

```
Command: zoom
All/.../<Scale(X/XP)>: [pick]
Other corner: [pick]
```

The text looks unattractive, like it was created by a computer! This is the basic font, called TXT, that is in every new AutoCAD drawing. Fortunately, AutoCAD comes with a large number of text fonts that look better than this one.

CHANGING THE TEXT FONT (Settings|Text Style)

Just like you have to load hatch patterns and linetypes into an AutoCAD drawing file, you also have to load additional text fonts.

1. Select **Settings|Text Style** from the menu bar.

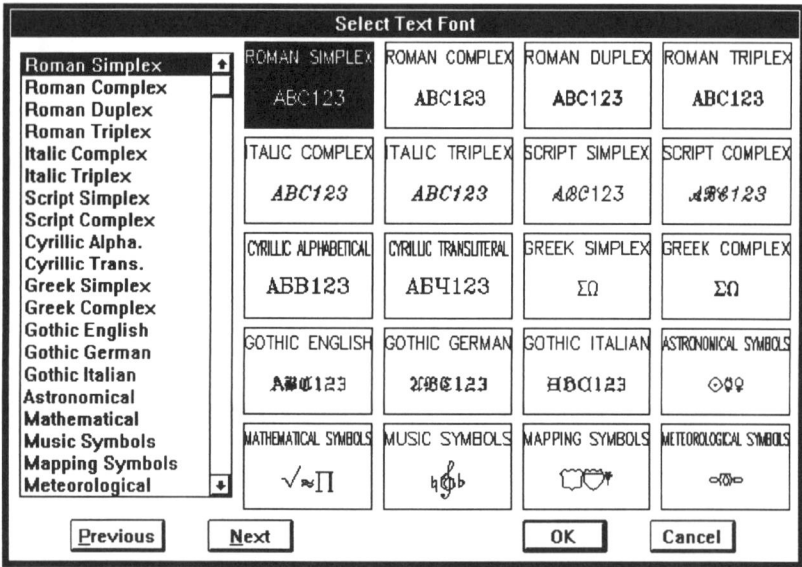

2. The Select Text Font icon menu appears on the screen. The menu displays 20 of AutoCAD LT's 42 fonts. As you see, some fonts are suitable for international projects; others are symbols.

3. Picking the **Next** button displays several fonts based on PostScript Type 1 PFB files supplied with AutoCAD LT. The Style command automatically converts any PostScript font file into AutoCAD's SHX font format.

4. Pick the **Previous** button to return to the first icon menu. Click on the **Roman Simplex** font. This is a clear and smooth-looking font that resembles the drafter's ISO text. Click on **OK** to dismiss the icon menu.

5. In the command prompt area, AutoCAD asks you a number of questions. These let you make subtle (and not so subtle) changes to the text font, which creates a text style. You can create many styles from a single font. AutoCAD automatically gives the style the same name as the font, RomanS (short for Roman Simplex).

   Text style name (or?): romans
   New style
   Font file <txt>: romans
   Height <0'-0">: **[Enter]**

Leave the style height at 0" by pressing Enter. A style height of 0" has a special meaning in AutoCAD. It means that you specify the height of the text later with the DText command. If you specify a height with the Style command, the height is fixed; you can no longer change it during the DText command.

6. Make the text a little bit narrower by specifying a width factor of 0.85, as follows:

   Width factor <1.00>: **.85**

The narrower width allows you to fit 15% more text into the same space, yet leaves the text perfectly legible.

7. Give an obliquing angle of 5 degrees, as follows:

   Obliquing angle <0.0000>: **5**

A slight forward slant of 5 degrees makes the text look a little nicer when plotted.

8. For the remaining questions answer Enter since you don't want the text to print backwards, upside-down or vertically:

   Backwards? <N> **[Enter]**
   Upside-down? <N> **[Enter]**
   Vertical? <N> **[Enter]**
   ROMANS is now the current text style.

You may have expected AutoCAD to change the word House to the new RomanS font. No such luck. That would have happened with the very early versions of AutoCAD, since old AutoCAD could only

Hour 5

handle one font in a drawing at a time. Nowadays, AutoCAD maintains as many fonts as you care to load into the drawing.

Instead, all text from now on is drawn with the RomanS font. To see this, add the call-out "Pool" to the pond. Later, you correct the mislabeled call-out.

9. First, save the current view with the View command. This makes it easier for you to later return to the same zoomed-in view. Select **View|View|Save** from the menu bar.
   Command: '_view
   ?/Delete/Restore/Save/Window: _save
   View name to save: **house**

10. Zoom out with the Zoom All command, then zoom into the pool with the Zoom Window command, as follows:
    Command: **z**
    All/.../<Scale(X/XP)>: **a**
    Regenerating drawing.
    Command: **[Enter]**
    ZOOM All/.../<Scale(X/XP)>: **[pick]**
    Other point: **[pick]**

11. Now that you see the pond area more clearly, start the DText command with **Draw|Text**. This time, use one of AutoCAD LT's six justification modes, as follows:
    Command: _text
    Justify/Style/<Start point>: **j**
    Align/Fit/Center/Middle/Right: **a**
    First text line point: **[pick one end of the pond]**
    Second text line point: **[pick other end of pond]**

Here you selected the Align justification, which draws text fitted between two points. All of AutoCAD LT's text justification modes are listed in the following table:

Justification	*Meaning*
Start point	Baseline left
Align	Fitted between two points
Fit	Fitted with constant text height
Center	Baseline center
Middle	Exact center of text
Right	Baseline right

Adding Notes and Dimensions

12. Since the Align option's pick points define the width and angle of the text, AutoCAD doesn't ask for the height or rotation angle. Instead, the Text command goes straight to the prompt:
    Text: **Pool**

The word "Pool" is drawn with the RomanS text style.

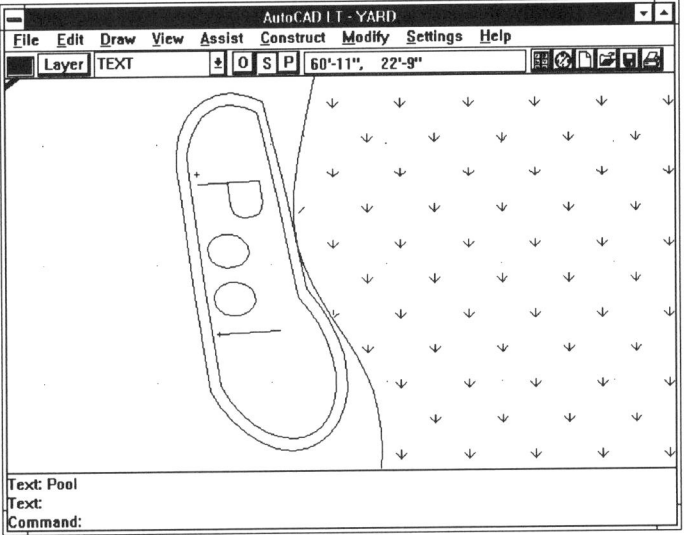

CHANGING EXISTING TEXT
(Modify|Edit Text, Edit|Rotate)

The word Pool is in the correct text style, but House isn't. To change the style of the word House, you use an unobvious aspect of the Change command.

1. First, return to the previously saved view. Select **View|View| Restore** and type "House", as follows:
   Command: _view
   ?/Delete/Restore/Save/Window: _restore
   View name to restore: **house**

81

Hour 5

2. Select **Modify|Change Point** and select the word House, as follows:

   Command: _change
   Select objects: **[pick House]**
   Select objects: **[Enter]**

3. After picking the word House, AutoCAD displays the following prompt:

   Properties/<Change point>: **[Enter]**

What is unobvious about the prompt is that when you press Enter, AutoCAD lets you change the characteristics of text (particularly when the menu pick reads "Change Point"!). Naturally, this only occurs if you have selected text to change.

4. Leave the text insertion point as is, but enter RomanS for the new text style name, as follows:

   Enter text insertion point: **[Enter]**
   New style or RETURN for no change: **romans**

AutoCAD redraws the word House in the RomanS font.

5. Press Enter for the remaining prompts:

   New height <2'-10">: **[Enter]**
   New rotation angle <0>: **[Enter]**
   New text <House>: **[Enter]**

6. Oops! "Pool" should read "Pond." If you need to change the wording of text, you use the DdEdit command, which is far more convenient than the Change command. Do a Zoom All to bring the word Pool back into view, as follows:

   Command: **z**
   All/.../<Scale(X/XP)>: **a**
   Regenerating drawing.

7. Select **Modify|Edit Text** and follow the prompts:

   Command: _ddedit
   <Select a TEXT or ATTDEF object>/Undo: **[pick Pool word]**

The Edit Text dialog box pops up on the screen.

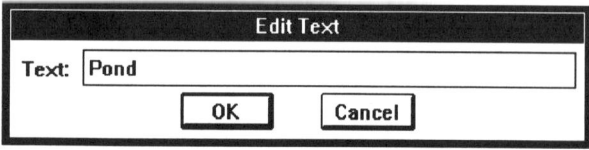

Adding Notes and Dimensions

8. Press the **Backspace** key and type **Pond**.
9. Pick the **OK** box at the bottom of the dialog box. AutoCAD instantly replaces "Pool" with "Pond."
10. Exit the DdEdit command by pressing Enter again:
    <Select a TEXT or ATTDEF object>/Undo: **[Enter]**
11. Now add some more text, such as the street name. Here we show how to write text sideways. Select **Draw|Text**, as follows:
    Command: _dtext
    Justify/Style/<Start point>: **[pick point on street]**
    Height <2'-10">: **[Enter]**
    Rotation angle <0.0000>: **90**
    Text: **Donlyn Avenue**
    Text: **[Enter]**

When you specify a rotation angle of 90 degrees, AutoCAD draws the text sideways.

12. If you picked the wrong rotation angle, you can rotate the text after the fact. Pick the text, as follows:
    Command: **[pick text]**
13. A blue box appears at the text's insertion point. Click on the blue box again so that it turns solid red.
14. Select the rotate option by pressing Enter twice until ** ROTATE ** shows up in the command prompt area. Then specify an angle of 180 degrees, as follows:
    ** STRETCH **
    <Stretch to point>/Base point/Copy/Undo/eXit: **[Enter]**
    ** MOVE **
    <Move to point>/Base point/Copy/Undo/eXit: **[Enter]**
    ** ROTATE **
    <Rotation angle>/Base point/Copy/Reference/eXit: **180**
15. AutoCAD draws the text flipped over. Press Ctrl+C twice to exit non-modal editing, then type "R" to clean up the screen with a redraw.
    Command: **[Ctrl]+C**
    Command: **[Ctrl]+C**
    Command: **r**
    REDRAW

Hour 5

As an alternative, you can use the mouse to show AutoCAD how you want the object rotated (as shown in the following illustration).

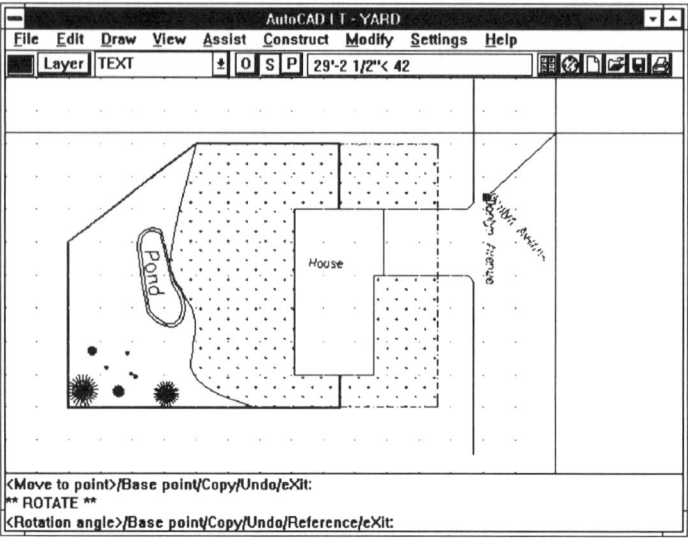

A FAST WAY TO PLACE TEXT

An advantage to DText command is that it lets you place text all over the drawing.

1. Use the DText command to add more call-outs to the drawing. Select **Draw|Text**, as follows:

   Command: _dtext
   Justify/Style/<Start point>: **[pick near bottom of drawing]**
   Height <2'-10">: **[Enter]**
   Rotation angle <90.0000>: **0**
   Text: **34486 Donlyn Avene**

Misspell "Avene" as shown; we correct it later. Notice the little square cursor displayed after each letter is drawn.

2. When you press Enter at the end of "Avene," the Text: prompt reappears. Now that you've noticed the spelling mistake in "Avene," you backspace with the Backspace key [BS] and type the correction, as follows:

   Text: **[BS][BS]ue**

3. Type the next line, as follows:
   Text: **Abbotsford BC**

You don't need to start the DText command again: DText automatically jumps to the next line below.

4. Now move the cursor near to a clump of trees and press the pick button. DText is ready for you to type more words:
   Text: **Birch trees**
   Text: **[move cursor to other trees] Western**
   Text: **Red Cedar**
   Text: **[Enter]**

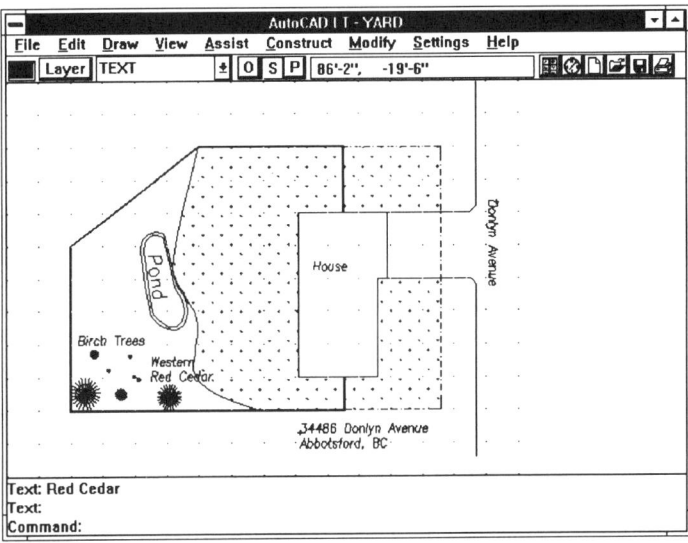

5. Press Enter one more time to end the DText command. When you do, AutoCAD rewrites all the text as left justified.

At this point, it is a good idea to save your work using the Save command.

REDUCING TEXT DISPLAY TIME (QText)

A lot of text in a drawing slows down the display speed. AutoCAD has a special command, called QText (short for Quick Text), that changes text into rectangular outlines.

Hour 5

1. Change the text into outlines with the Qtext command. Select **Settings|Drawing Aids** and AutoCAD displays the Drawing Aids dialog box.
2. Click on the check box next to **Quick Text**, located in the Modes column.
3. Click on the **OK** button. The call-outs look no different! AutoCAD doesn't change the text until the next regeneration.
4. Force a screen regeneration with the Regen command. Select **View|Regen** and the text turns into a rectangle.

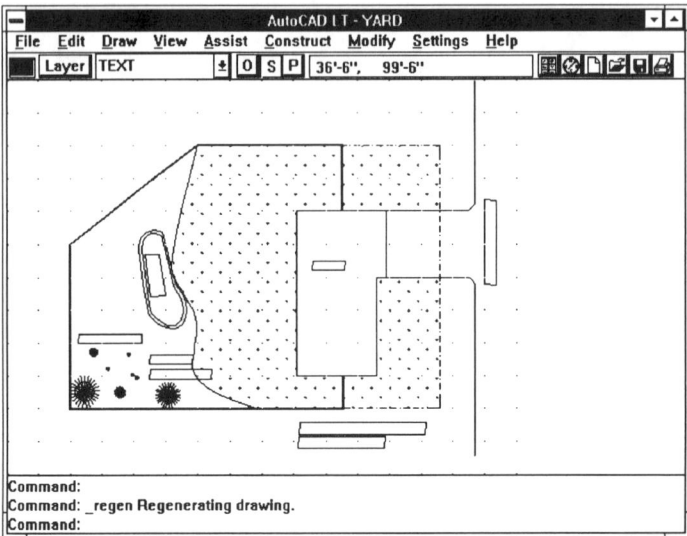

5. Change the outlines back to text, this time typing the QText command followed by the Regen command, as follows:

    Command: **qtext**
    ON/OFF <On>: **off**
    Command: **regen**
    Regenerating drawing.

DIMENSIONING THE YARD (DimScale)

With several call-outs placed on the drawing, you may want to add dimensions to the lot. This is done with the Dim (short for dimensioning) command, one of the most involved commands of AutoCAD's repertoire. Fortunately, AutoCAD comes preconfigured with most dimensioning variables set to reasonable values. Most of the time, you only need to set one variable, the scale of the dimensions.

1. First, set the dimensioning scale by typing the DimScale command, which is easier than navigating a number of dialog boxes. The dimension scale ensures that the arrow heads and text are drawn a size appropriate for the drawing. Start the DimScale command, as follows:

   Command: **dimscale**

2. For a dimension scale of 1.0, AutoCAD draws the dimensioning text 0.18" high, which is close to 3/16". However, as you saw with the Text command, the text needs to be large enough to be legible when plotted. To find the new value of Dimscale, divide the plotted text height by the default text height, as follows:

   Plotted text height   34"
   ------------------------ =   ------- = 188.89
   Default text height   0.18"

Thus, the value of the dimension scale should be about 190, as follows:

   New value for DIMSCALE <1.0000>: **190**

3. Since all of the lot dimensioning takes place at intersections, turn on INTersection object snap mode, as follows:

   Command: **osnap**
   Object snap modes: **int**

HORIZONTAL AND CONTINUOUS DIMENSIONS (Draw|Linear Dimensions)

1. To dimension the drawing, select **Draw|Linear Dimensions** from the menu bar.

   Command: _dim1
   Dim: _horizontal

AutoCAD changes the prompt from Command: to Dim: to remind you that you are in dimensioning mode. No AutoCAD commands work while the Dim: prompt appears except those relating to dimensioning and transparent commands.

2. Dimension the lower lot line, as follows:

Hour 5

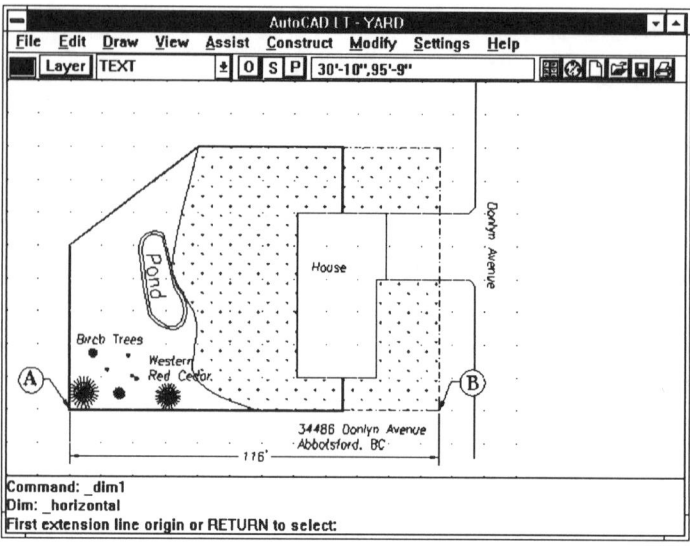

First extension line origin or RETURN to select: **[pick A]**
Second extension line origin: **[pick B]**
Dimension line location (Text/Angle): **[pick below the lot line]**
Dimension text <116'>: **[Enter]**

Press Enter at the Dimension text prompt; AutoCAD knows the length of the line and reports it in the angle brackets. If you like, you can type in any other dimension or text. AutoCAD automatically draws all the components of the dimension.

2. Try another horizontal dimension, this time along the top of the lot line. Select **Draw|Linear Dimensions|Horizontal** again.

   Command: _dim1
   Dim: _horizontal
   First extension line origin or RETURN to select: **[pick A]**
   Second extension line origin: **[pick B]**
   Dimension line location: **[pick]**
   Dimension text <40'>: **[Enter]**

Notice how AutoCAD draws the extension lines long enough to reach your pick points.

Adding Notes and Dimensions

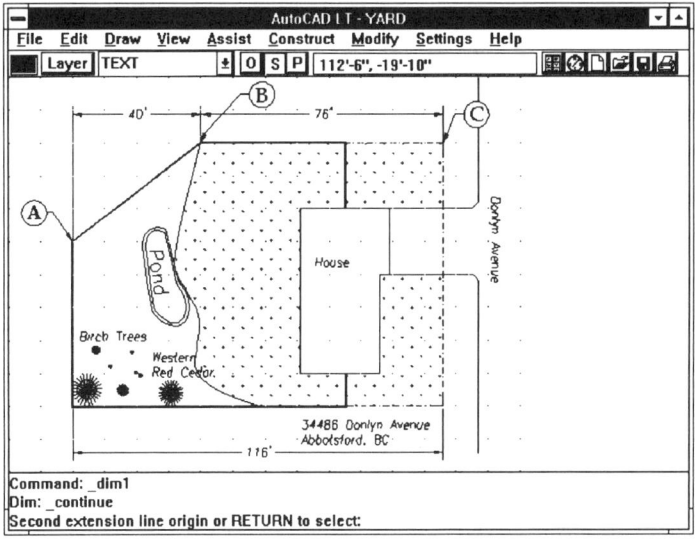

3. Continue the horizontal dimension with the Continue command. Select **Draw|Linear Dimensions|Continue**.

   Command: _dim1
   Dim: _continuous
   Second extension line origin or RETURN to select: **[pick C]**
   Dimension text (Text/Angle) <76'>: **[Enter]**

Since AutoCAD knows where your last extension line was, it only needs to know the location of the next extension line to draw in the second dimension.

VERTICAL AND BASELINE DIMENSIONS

1. To draw a vertical dimension, select **Draw|Linear Dimensions| Vertical**.

89

Hour 5

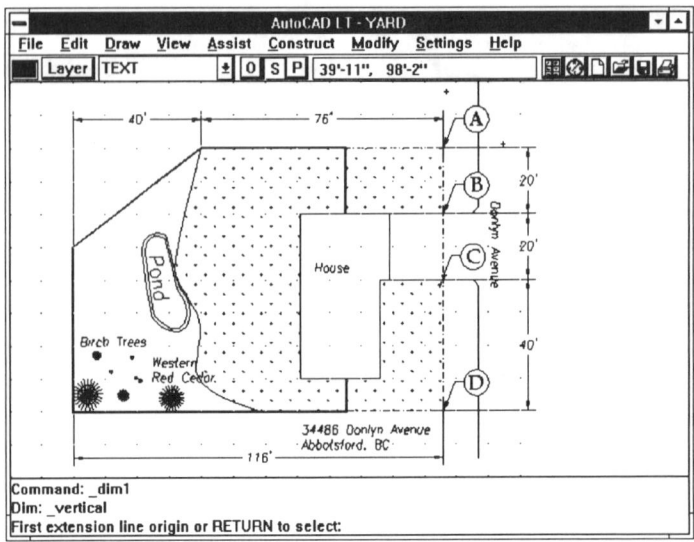

```
Command: _dim1
Dim: _vertical
First extension line origin or RETURN to select: [pick A]
Second extension line origin: [pick B]
Dimension line location (Text/Angle): [pick]
Dimension text <20'>: [Enter]
```

2. Use the **Continue** command to continue the vertical dimensions along the right side of the lot at points C and D.

3. A variation on the Continue command is the Baseline command. Rather than continue a dimension from the previous extension line, Baseline dimensions from the original extension line.

Adding Notes and Dimensions

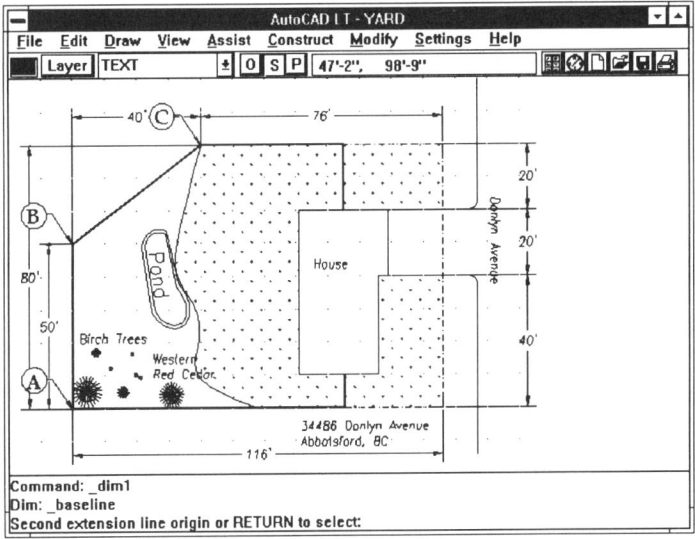

```
Command: _dim1
Dim: _vertical
First extension line origin or RETURN to select: [pick A]
Second extension line origin: [pick B]
Dimension line location: [pick]
Dimension text (Text/Angle) <50'>: [Enter]
```

4. Try the Baseline command. Select **Draw|Linear Dimensions| Baseline**.

```
Command: _dim1
Dim: _baseline
Second extension line origin or RETURN to select: [pick C]
Dimension text (Text/Angle) <80'>: [Enter]
```

The Baseline and Continue commands work with horizontal, vertical, and angled dimensions.

ALIGNED AND RADIAL DIMENSIONS
(Draw|Radial Dimensions)

So far, you have dimensioned the angled portion of the lot line with horizontal and vertical dimension commands. To dimension an angled line, you use the Aligned command.

1. Select **Draw|Linear Dimensions|Aligned**.

91

Hour 5

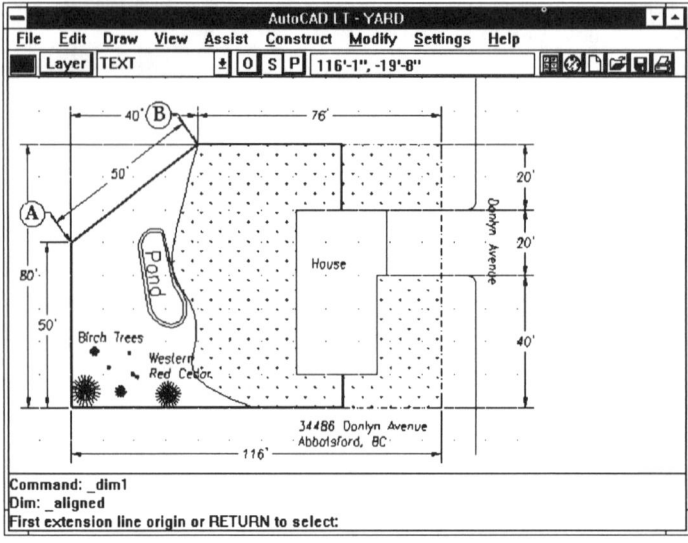

```
Command: _dim1
Dim: _aligned
First extension line origin or RETURN to select: [pick A]
Second extension line origin: [pick B]
Dimension line location: [pick]
Dimension text (Text/Angle) <50'>: [Enter]
```

2. The dimensioning commands you have been using present pretty much the same prompts to you. Now try some dimension commands that are a bit different. For example, the Radius command dimensions an arc or circle that you pick. Select **Draw|Radial Dimensions|Radius**, as follows:

```
Command: _dim1
Dim: _radius
Select arc or circle: [pick a driveway radius]
Dimension text (Text/Angle) <3'>: [Enter]
Enter leader length for text: [pick a suitable point]
```

The Radius command gives you some flexibility as to where you want to place the dimension text. As you move the cursor, AutoCAD ghosts in the leader and text.

Adding Notes and Dimensions

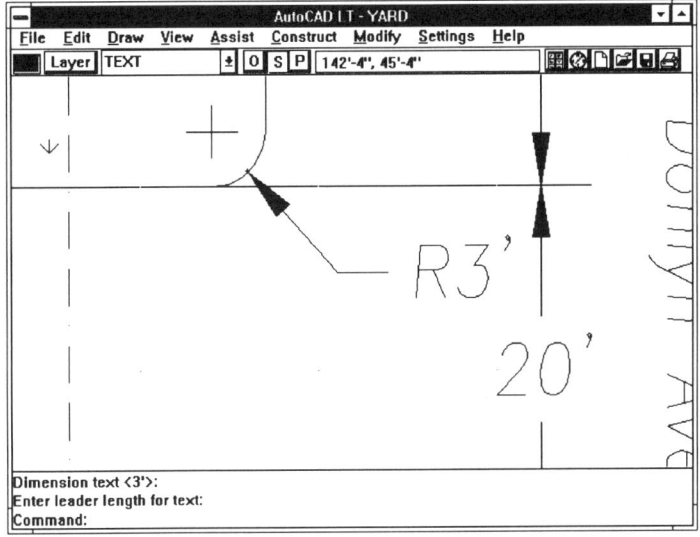

Remember to save your drawing and plot out the final version (see figure below).

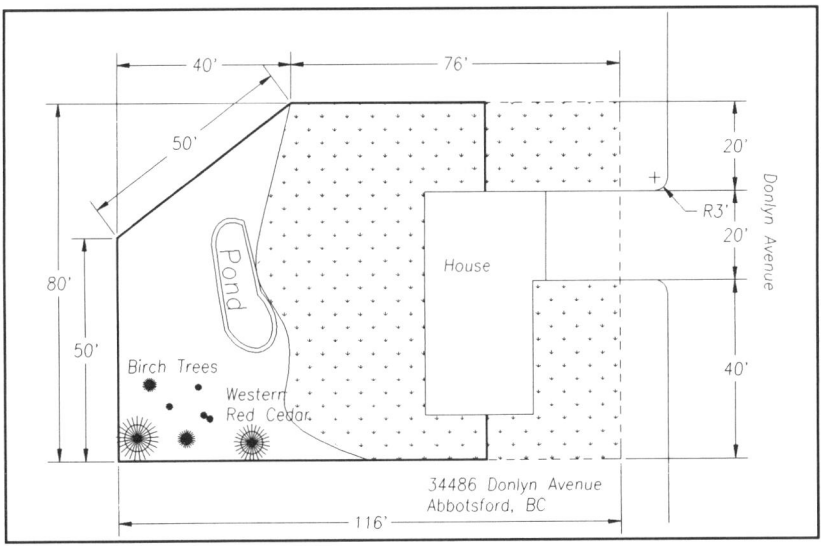

In this hour, you learned how to add call-outs to the drawing, dimension the yard, and insert a border around the drawing. This concludes the lessons on drawing in two dimensions. Next hour, you learn how to create a symbol library for more efficient work.

93

Hour 6
CREATING SYMBOLS AND ATTRIBUTES

INTRODUCTION

In the first part of this book, you learned how to draw and edit an accurate drawing with AutoCAD LT. In the second part of this book, you learn what differentiates CAD from other drawing programs: creating custom symbols with embedded information and automating the design process.

The purpose for using symbols in a drawing is two-fold: (1) symbols make you a faster drafter; (2) symbols store customized information, called "attributes." As you find out in this hour, it is much faster to add a symbol to a drawing than draw the symbol from scratch each time you need it. While you could use the Copy command to repeat a symbol without redrawing it, adding a symbol is more efficient than simply copying it. A drawing that uses symbols takes up less disk space. Using symbols makes you a faster drafter; if you are a faster drafter, you complete more work in the same amount of time—or finish work sooner.

Later this hour, you learn how to create attributes, add them to the symbols, and store the symbols on disk. When it comes time to produce a bill of materials of the drawing, AutoCAD automatically produces a list of all the symbols in the drawing; you can't do that with the Copy command!

Creating Symbols and Attributes

BEFORE YOU BEGIN

The example used for the design portion of this book creates a drawing of part of the electrical schematic of an automobile. If you have a repair manual for your automobile, you can reproduce your own schematic with AutoCAD.

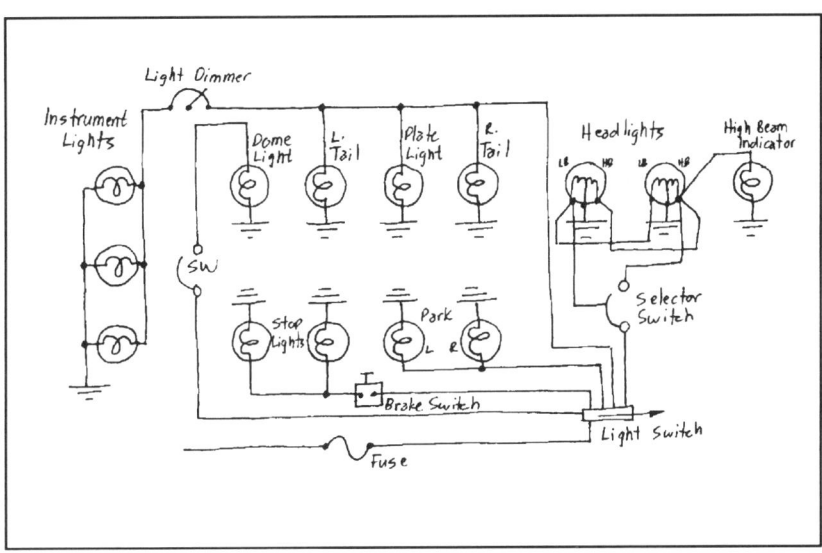

If you'd rather not, follow along with the schematic sketch above, which is the drawing used by this book.

PREPARING FOR DRAWING THE SYMBOLS

To create a drawing with custom symbols takes three steps: (1) start a new drawing and create the custom symbols; (2) save the symbols to disk; (3) create the new drawing using the symbols. AutoCAD calls symbols "blocks," which is the name we use from now on. (Other CAD packages call symbols "components," "cells," or "parts.")

1. Start AutoCAD LT by double-clicking on its icon in the Windows Program Manager.
2. Create a new drawing with the name "SYMBOLS." Select **File|New** from the menu bar. Type **SYMBOLS** as the new drawing name, then click on the **OK** button.

95

3. Since you will be drawing to an accuracy of 0.1 units, select **Settings|Drawings Aids** from the menu bar. When the Drawing Aids dialog box appears:
   - Turn **Ortho** mode on by clicking the check box.
   - Turn **Snap** on.
   - Set the snap spacing to 0.1.
   - Turn **Grid** on.
   - Ensure that the grid spacing is set to 0.0.

   Click **OK** when done. The screen fills with a fine grid of dots.

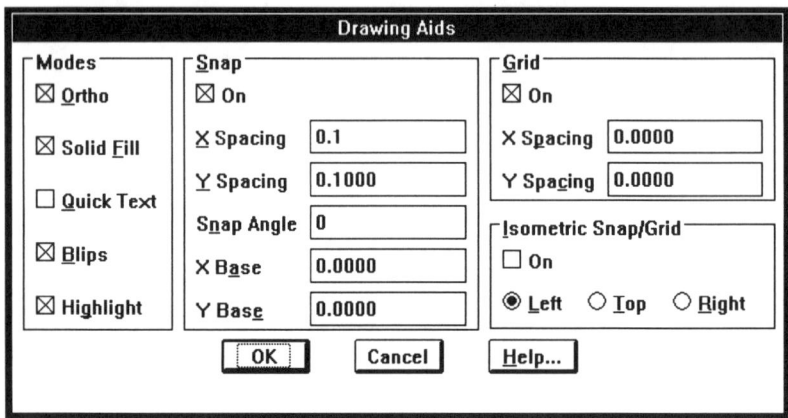

4. Change the coordinate display from absolute units to relative units. Click on the coordinate readout display box on the toolbar twice. A relative coordinate displays the x,y-distance from the last picked point to the current cursor location. That makes it easier to design the components.

SELECTING THE COMPONENTS

Before drawing the first component, look at the sketch of the schematic and decide which parts should be converted into components. The light bulbs are likely candidates since there are so many of them. Other candidates are the headlamps and the ground symbols.

Any part should be drawn as a component that you might need to list in the bill of material, even if it appears only once: the dome light switch, the fuse, the instrument light dimmer, the light switch, the brake light switch, even the solder connections.

The figure below shows the blocks needed for the electrical schematic. The small black dot on each block shows its insertion point (more later this hour).

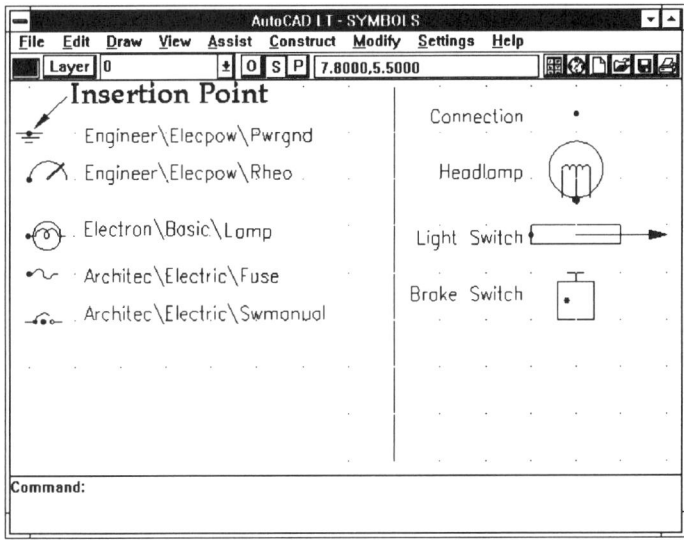

The six symbols on the left-hand side of the figure above come with the AutoCAD LT package, which includes 374 symbols. When the software was installed on your computer's hard disk, a subdirectory was created named \acltwin\symbol. This subdirectory contains four more subdirectories that group the symbols into disciplines: Architec (architectural symbols), Business, Electron (electronic symbols), and Engineer.

Each of these four subdirectories is further divided into subdirectories, each of which contain between six and 43 symbols stored as WMF files, as the following table illustrates:

Hour 6

Architec	Business	Electron	Engineer
Bathroom	Clipart	Basic	Elecpow
Cabinets	Flowchrt		Fastener
Electric	LANs		GPT
Framing	Maps		Hydraulc
Furnish			Strcstel
General			Welding
HVAC			
Kitchen			
Landscpe			
Office			
Plumbing			
Sinks			

With the drawing set up, you begin drawing the remaining four symbols (on the righthand side of the figure, above). Blocks, or symbols, are usually drawn at unit size. "Unit size" means that the entire component is drawn within a 1-inch square boundary. That makes it much easier to scale the component when it comes time to place it in the drawing.

DRAWING THE FIRST SYMBOL (Draw|Donut)

To start drawing components, begin with the easiest symbol, the symbol for the connection.

1. Enlarge the drawing area with the **View|Zoom|Window** command.
2. The dot for the connection is drawn with the Donut command, which draws solid-filled and thick-walled circles. Select **Draw|Donut** from the menu bar.
3. AutoCAD prompts you for the size of the donut, as follows:
   Command: _donut
   Inside diameter <0.5000>: **0**
   Outside diameter <1.0000>: **0.1**
4. AutoCAD prompts you to place the donut, as follows:
   Center of donut: **[pick]**
   Center of donut: **[Enter]**

Creating Symbols and Attributes

The Donut command automatically repeats itself until you end it by pressing Enter.

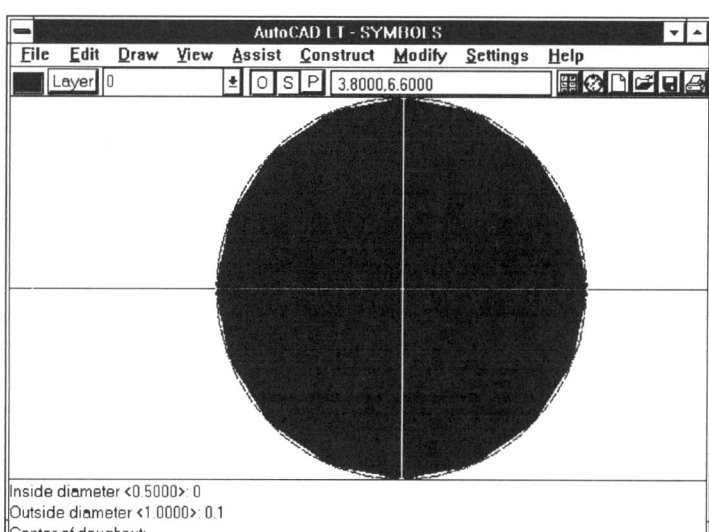

CREATING THE ATTRIBUTE FIELDS
(Construct|Define Attribute)

With the connection symbol drawn, you now create the attribute fields. Attributes are customized descriptions of symbols; attributes attach to only blocks. While the drawing shows you how to assemble the electrical system, the attribute list tells you how many parts are needed for the assembly, the total cost, and so on.

The connection symbol is a graphical symbol. It and other symbols are a collection of dots, circles, and lines that represent physical parts of the automotive electrical system.

Just as the block is a graphical description of the ground symbol, the attribute is the textual description. The attribute information describes its part number, the manufacturer, the price, and any other information you want to include.

You can create descriptive labels such as "Product name," "Manufacturer," "Model number," "Stock number," "Serial number," and "Material." (You could include "Price" as an attribute

Hour 6

field but, since prices change so frequently, it is better to deal with the price later in the spreadsheet program. Instead, use "Price" with a price code.)

The analogy is to a database program, where each attribute is a record and each record has fields. Each AutoCAD attribute field has up to 256 characters. Although you can store 256 fields (for a total of 64KB of information) in each block, you probably find that you rarely take advantage of that much space.

1. For the connection symbol, you create an attribute with the DdAttDef (short for attribute definition) command. Select **Construct|Define Attribute** from the menu bar. AutoCAD displays the Attribute Definition dialog box.

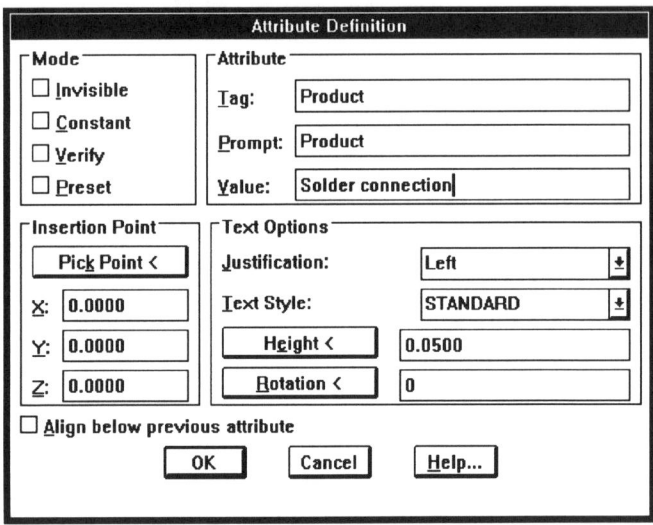

Although the dialog box has 15 separate fields to fill in, we work with just five: the Attribute section, the Insertion Point, and the Text Height.

2. Fill in the following data in the Attribute section:
   Tag: **Product**
   Prompt: **Product**
   Value: **Solder connection**

"Tag" is an identifier used by AutoCAD and you to identify the attribute.

"Prompt" is the prompt displayed by AutoCAD when you place the block in the drawing. Don't include a colon (:) at the end; AutoCAD does that for you.

"Value" is the default value later displayed by AutoCAD in angle brackets, as follows:

Product <Solder connection>:

The default value is anything from a specific value to a filler. You use a specific value, such as "Solder connection," if it is a common value, as in this example of the connection. Using "Solder connection" as the default saves you many keystrokes.

You would use a filler to remind yourself (and other users) the size and type of the field. For example, "99999" suggests a five-digit number; "AAA-999" indicates three characters followed by a dash, followed by three digits.

3. Set the text height to a small, unobtrusive value, such as 0.05.
4. Select the insertion point by clicking on the **Pick Point** button. AutoCAD prompts, as follows:
   Command: _ddattdef
   Start point: **[pick right edge of donut]**

This places the attribute data to the right of the connection block.

5. AutoCAD returns the dialog box. Click the **OK** button.
6. Add a second attribute directly below the first. Press the Spacebar to repeat the DdAttDef command, as follows:
   Command: **[Spacebar]**
   _DDATTDEF
7. When the Attribute Definition dialog box appears, click the check box next to **Align below previous attribute**. This ensures the second attribute lines up with the first one.
8. Fill in the following data in the Attribute section:
   Tag: **Stockno**
   Prompt: **Stock No.**
   Value: **000-0000**

Ensure the tag name "Stockno" is a single word, with no spaces.

101

Hour 6

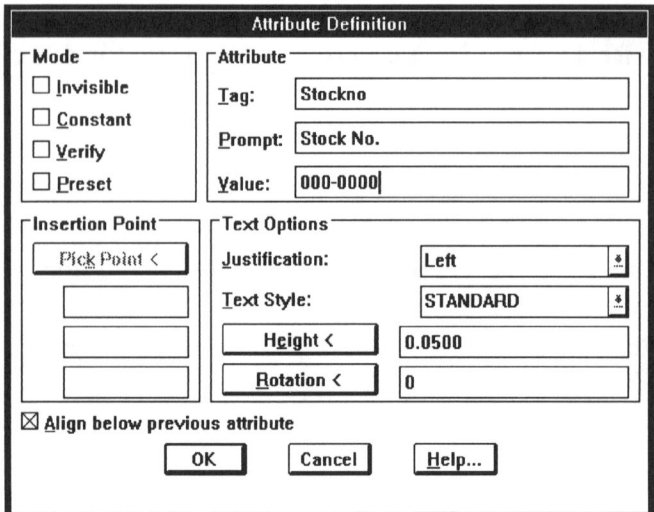

9. Click on the **OK** button and AutoCAD adds the second attribute.

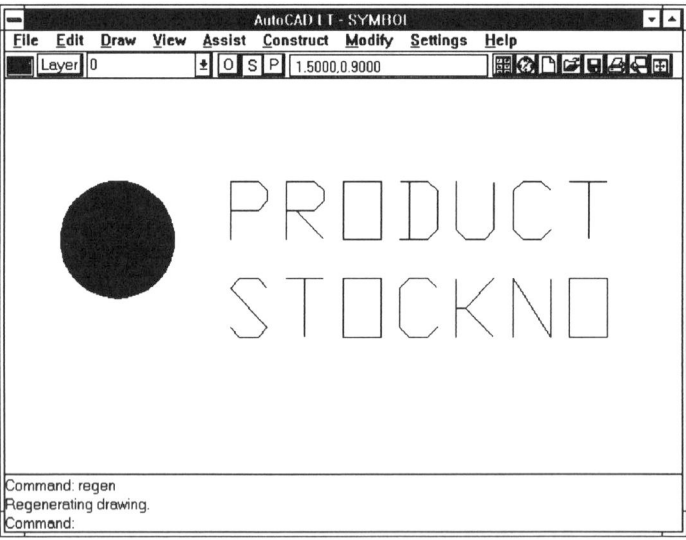

COMBINING THE SYMBOL AND ATTRIBUTE INTO A BLOCK

What you have now is the donut and the two attributes (defined by the tag names "PRODUCT" and "STOCKNO"). The final step is to link the donut and attributes together into a single block.

1. Turn the donut and attributes into a block with the BMake command by selecting **Construct|Make Block** from the menu bar.
2. When the Block Definition dialog box appears, name the block "CONNECT."
3. Click on the **Select Objects** button and select the donut and attribute, as follows:

   Command: _bmake
   Select objects: **c**
   First corner: **[pick]**
   Other corner: **[pick]**
   3 found
   Select objects: **[Enter]**

4. The Base Point is also known as the "insertion point," which is where the block is placed in the drawing. When deciding on the insertion point, pick a convenient spot such as the center of the connection point.

Change the Base Point from (0,0,0) to the center of the donut. Click on the **Select Point** button and select the center of the donut with the CENter object snap, as follows:

   Insertion base point: **cen**
   of **[pick donut]**

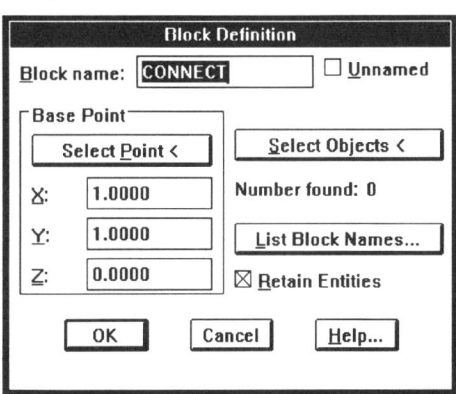

5. Click on the **OK** button.
6. AutoCAD has stored the donut as a block definition in the drawing. Practice placing the block with the DdInsert command. Select **Draw|Insert Block** from the menu bar. AutoCAD displays the Insert dialog box.

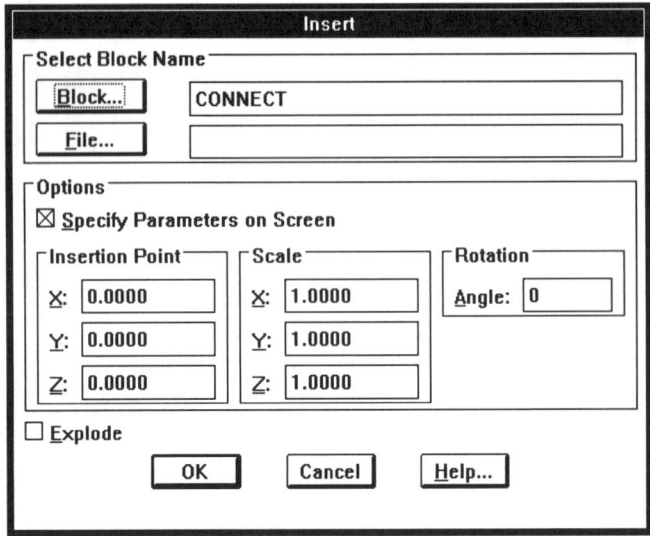

7. Type **CONNECT** as the Block name, then click the **OK** button.
8. The dialog box disappears and AutoCAD prompts you, as follows:

   Command: _ddinsert
   Insertion point: **[pick]**

Pick any convenient point on the screen. As you move the mouse, AutoCAD moves an outlined image of the connection dot on the screen.

   X scale factor <1>/Corner/XYZ: **[Enter]**
   Y scale factor (default=X): **[Enter]**
   Rotation angle <0>: **[Enter]**

You can supply a scale factor or indicate the size by typing C for corner. For this example, press Enter to draw the connection block 0.1 units in diameter. Press Enter again to keep the donut round and at zero degrees rotation.

Creating Symbols and Attributes

9. When you placed the tree block in Hour 3, there were no attributes attached and this would have ended the DdInsert command. Since the Connect block has attributes, the AutoCAD prompts continue, as follows:

   Enter attribute values
   PRODUCT <Solder Connection>: **[Enter]**
   STOCK NO. <000-0000>: **[Enter]**

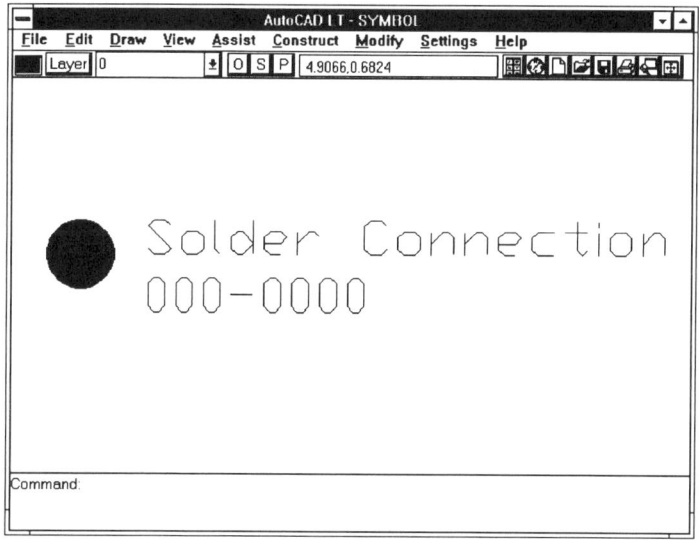

AutoCAD draws the connection block accompanied by the words "Solder Connection" and "000-0000."

STORING BLOCKS ON DISK
(File|Import/Export|Block Out)

The connection block is stored in the Symbols drawing. Let's store a copy of the block as a file on disk with the WBlock command. By placing a copy of the block on disk, all other AutoCAD drawings share the block.

1. Select **File|Import/Export|Block Out** from the menu bar. AutoCAD displays the Create Drawing File dialog box.

105

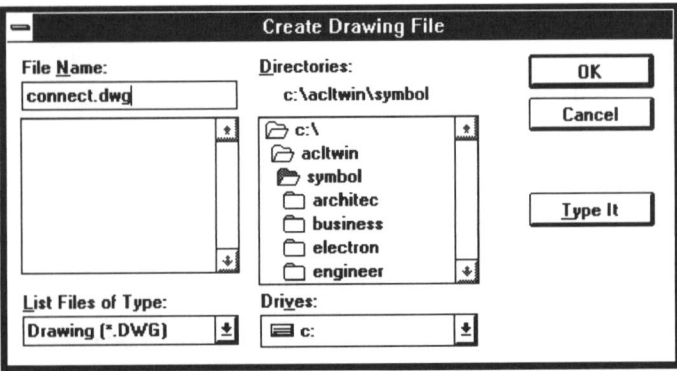

2. Ensure the subdirectory is \acltwin\symbol. Type the File Name **connect** and click on the **OK** button.

3. AutoCAD redundantly asks you for the block's name, as follows:
   Command: _wblock
   Block name: **connect**

You now have two copies of the Connect block: (1) in the drawing symbol; and (2) stored on disk as connect.dwg.

Congratulations! You've worked your way through the somewhat complicated process of creating and attaching attributes. You now load the six blocks supplied in AutoCAD LT's symbol library.

LOADING BLOCKS FROM DISK (FILE|IMPORT/EXPORT|WMF IN)

Since AutoCAD LT supplies its symbol library in WMF format (short for Windows Metafile), we cannot place one of the symbols directly into the drawing with the Insert or DdInsert commands. Instead, we have to "import" the symbol with the Wmf In command, which translates the symbol from WMF format to AutoCAD's own DWG format.

1. Select **File|Import/Export|Wmf In** from the menu bar.
2. AutoCAD displays the Import WMF dialog box. Navigate down to the \acltwin\symbol\architec\electric subdirectory and click on **fuse.wmf** to preview it.

Creating Symbols and Attributes

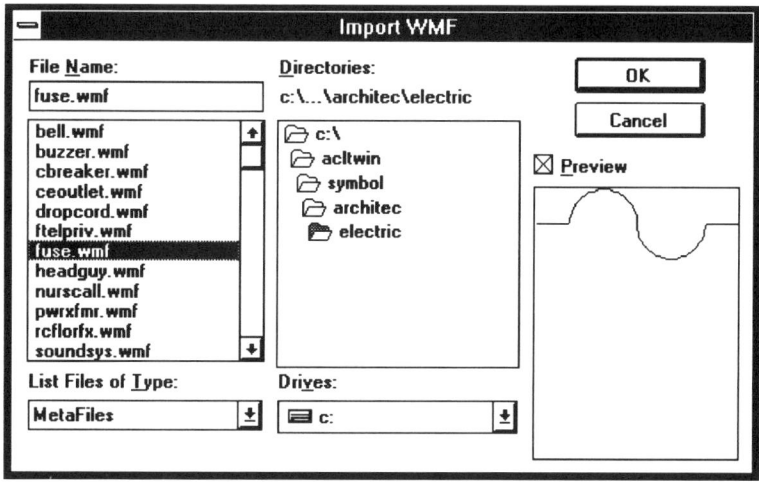

3. Click on the **OK** button to load the drawing into AutoCAD.
4. After AutoCAD converts the WMF file into DWG format, it places it into the drawing as a block, as follows:

   Command: _wmfin
   _INSERT Block name (or ?) <CONNECT>: WMF1
   Insertion point: **[pick]**
   X scale factor <1>/Corner/XYZ: **[Enter]**
   Y scale factor (default=X): **[Enter]**
   Rotation angle <0>: **[Enter]**

5. AutoCAD places the symbol in the drawing at an arbitrary scale. Use the Scale command to reduce the symbol so that its width is 1.0 units wide.
6. Create the following attributes for the fuse with the Attdef command:

   Tag: **Product**
   Prompt: **Product**
   Value: **40 Amp fuse**

   Tag: **Stockno**
   Prompt: **Stock No.**
   Value: **300-0040**

7. Combine the fuse and the two attributes into a single block with the name **fuse40** with the Block command.

107

8. Save the fuse block to disk as **fuse40.dwg** with the WBlock command.

CREATING THE OTHER BLOCKS

Create eight other blocks with attributes for the electrical schematic. Following are the names you give them, along with tips for drawing the bits and pieces:

Dome Switch is the supplied swmanual.dwg symbol found in subdirectory \acltwin\symbol\architec\electric.

>Block name: **DomeSw**
>
>Tag: **Product**
>Prompt: **Product**
>Value: **Single-pole switch**
>
>Tag: **Stockno**
>Prompt: **Stock No.**
>Value: **200-0020**

Light Bulb is the supplied lamp.dwg found in subdirectory \acltwin\symbol\electron\basic.

>Block name: **LBulb**
>
>Tag: **Product**
>Prompt: **Product**
>Value: **Single**
>
>Tag: **Stockno**
>Prompt: **Stock No.**
>Value: **400-0001**

Instrument Light Dimmer is the supplied rheo.dwg found in subdirectory \acltwin\symbol\engineer\elecpow.

>Block name: **LDimmer**
>
>Tag: **Product**
>Prompt: **Product**
>Value: **80 Ohm dimmer**

Creating Symbols and Attributes

Tag: **Stockno**
Prompt: **Stock No.**
Value: **500-0080**

Ground is the supplied pwrgnd.dwg found in subdirectory \acltwin\symbol\engineer\elecpow.

Block name: **Ground**

Tag: **Product**
Prompt: **Product**
Value: **Lug and Screw Ground**

Tag: **Stockno**
Prompt: **Stock No.**
Value: **100-0001**

Headlamp is drawn with circles, arcs, lines, and donuts (see figure below).

Block name: **HLamp**

Tag: **Product**
Prompt: **Product**
Value: **Dual beam headlamp**

Tag: **Stockno**
Prompt: **Stock No.**
Value: **400-0220**

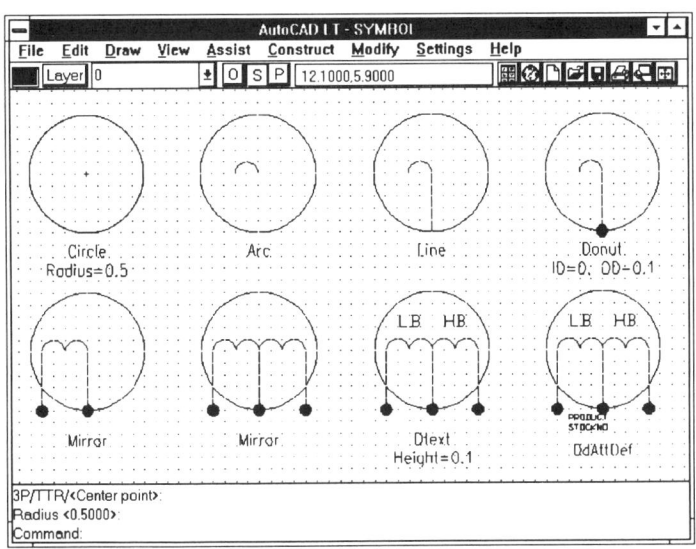

109

1. Turn on ortho mode; set snap and grid to 0.1.
2. Draw a 1-inch circle with the **Draw|Circle|Center,Radius** command, setting the radius to 0.5 inches.
3. The **Draw|Arc|Start,Center,End** command draws one filament arc.
4. You use the **Draw|Line** command to extend the center filament to the base of the lamp.
5. Place a 0.1 diameter donut at the end of the line.
6. Use the **Construct|Mirror** command to make a mirrored copy of the line, donut, and arc to the left.
7. Repeat the Mirror command to make a second copy to the left.
8. The **Draw|Text** command adds the HB (short for high beam) and LB (low beam) text. Use center justification and a text height of 0.1.
9. Finally, use the BMake command to convert the drawing into a block called "HLamp." Select the center donut as the reference point.

Light Switch is drawn with the Rectang rectangle command 1" x 0.2" in size. Add a line with the Line command. Draw the 0.3-long arrowhead with the PLine command, setting the starting width to 0.0 and the ending width to 0.2.

Block name: **LSwitch**

Tag: **Product**
Prompt: **Product**
Value: **Four-pole switch**

Tag: **Stockno**
Prompt: **Stock No.**
Value: **200-0440**

Brake Light Switch is drawn with the Polygon command, using the Edge option (0.4 units long). Finish with the Line and Donut commands.

Block name: **BSwitch**

Tag: **Product**
Prompt: **Product**
Value: **Single pole brake switch**

Creating Symbols and Attributes

Tag: **Stockno**
Prompt: **Stock No.**
Value: **200-0510**

Now store each symbol on disk with the WBlock command. Store the files in the \aclt\symbols subdirectory so they don't overwrite the original symbols located in the other subdirectories.

Finally, save the Symbols drawing. For easy reference to your new symbol library, plot the drawing.

DRAWING THE ELECTRICAL SCHEMATIC (Draw|Insert Block)

With the ten electrical blocks stored on disk, you now create the drawing of the automobile electrical schematic.

1. With **File|New**, start a new drawing named ELECTRIC. Make sure Ortho mode is turned on; set snap to 0.1 and grid to 0.5.
2. AutoCAD lets you place blocks in the drawing in two ways: (1) the first time you need a symbol, load it from disk; and (2) for each subsequent placement, insert the block from the definition stored in the drawing.

Begin placing the symbols with the **Draw|Insert Block** command. AutoCAD displays the Insert dialog box.

3. Click on the **File** button to load a block from the hard drive. AutoCAD displays the Select Drawing File dialog box.
4. If necessary, navigate down to the \acltwin\symbol subdirectory. Double-click on **fuse40.dwg** to load it.
5. AutoCAD continues with the usual insert prompts, as follows:
   Command: _ddinsert
   Insertion point: **[pick]**
   X scale factor <1>/Corner/XYZ: **[Enter]**
   Y scale factor (default=X): **[Enter]**
   Rotation angle <0>: **[Enter]**
6. Insert the other symbols as blocks, placing them in roughly the correct location.

Hour 6

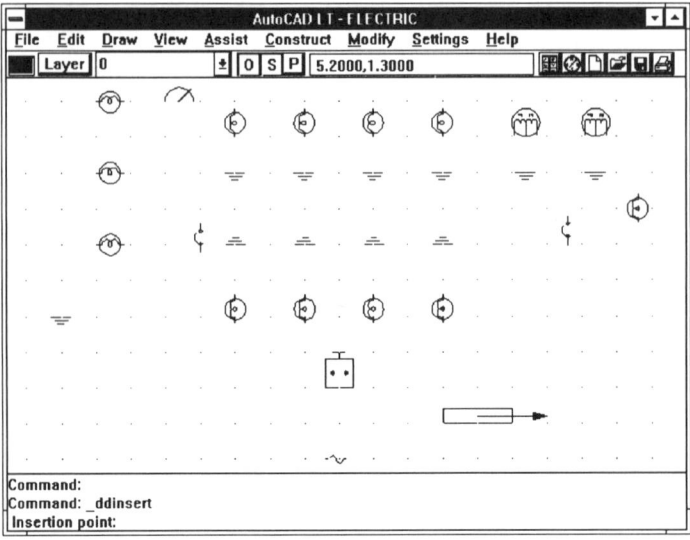

7. Turn on Ortho mode and ENDpoint object snap. Use the **Draw|Line** command to connect the blocks, as shown below. Make liberal use of the Aerial View window to get a better view of your work.

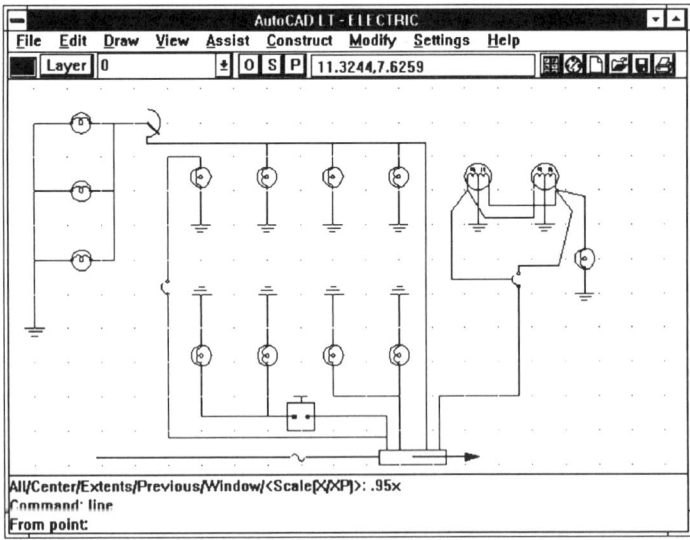

8. Complete the electrical connections by placing the Connect block.

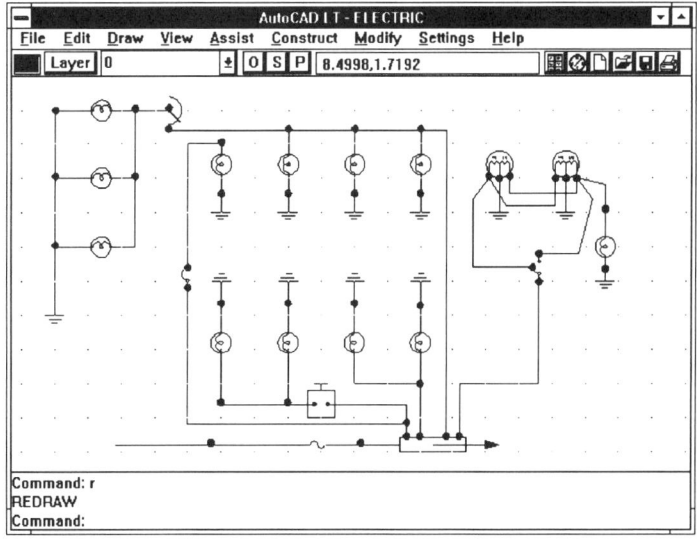

9. Add descriptive text to the schematic with the DText command.
10. Finally, save your work, then plot it out, as shown below.

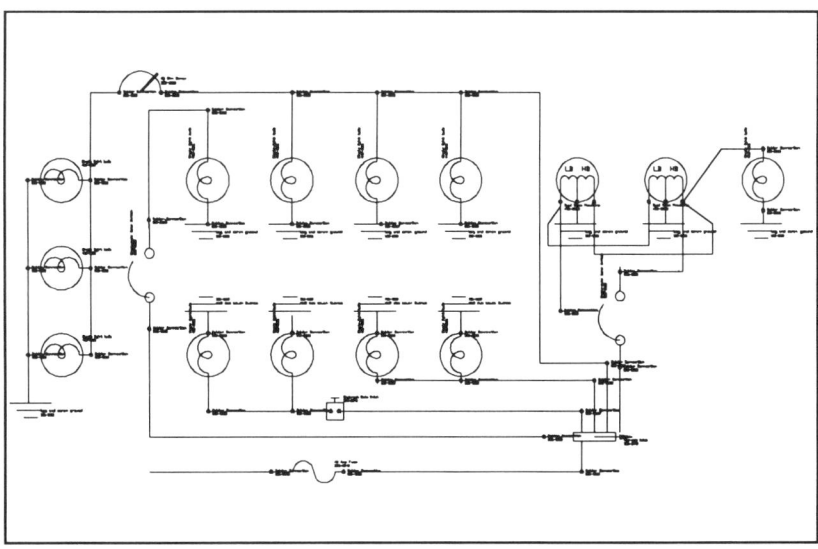

Hour 6

In this hour, you learned how to create efficient symbols and use some of the 374 symbols supplied with AutoCAD LT. You also learned how to create attributes and attach them to blocks. Finally, you created your own custom symbol library with the WBlock command.

In the next chapter, you learn how to extract the attribute data from the drawing.

Hour 7
BILLS OF MATERIAL

INTRODUCTION

In the last hour, you learned how to create a custom symbol library with AutoCAD. In this chapter, you learn how to extract the attribute information with AutoCAD LT's AttExt (short for attribute extract) command. It also provides a link to spreadsheet and database programs for further processing.

Last hour, you created the drawing ELECTRIC of an automobile electrical schematic. The drawing contains many components: a couple of headlamps, a fuse, several light bulbs, and quite a few ground and solder connections. You could count the components by hand but you would probably miscount them. It's faster and more accurate to let AutoCAD count the components for you.

Autodesk has made no effort to make the process intuitive (in fact, the AttExt command reckons back to AutoCAD v 2.0 for DOS and has not changed since 1985). That is, you probably can't run AttExt without being shown the steps to follow, unlike other Windows programs that boast "coaches" and "wizards" to step you through complicated procedures. The three steps required are:

1. Create an attribute-extract template file.
2. Set up the AttExt command to extract attributes.
3. Import attribute data into a spreadsheet.

STEP 1: CREATE ATTRIBUTE EXTRACT TEMPLATE FILE

For AutoCAD to extract attribute data, it needs to know which data you want extracted and the format you want the data in. Unfortunately, AutoCAD has no default values; you must create a "template" file that the AttExt command refers to.

1. If necessary, start Windows.
2. Start the Notepad application, a text editor that ships with every copy of Windows.
3. Type the text shown in the figure into Notepad. Make sure you type the number 0 (zero) and not the letter O in the right column.

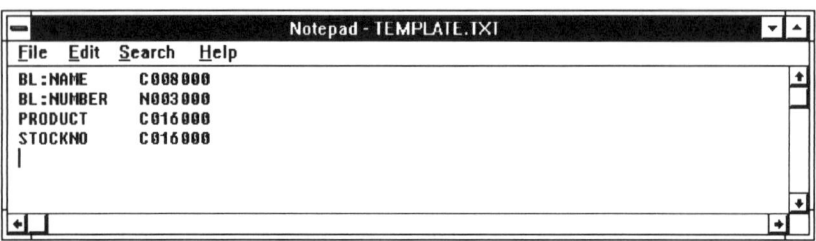

4. Save the template file as TEMPLATE.TXT.

The text in the template file has the following meaning:

Template file	Meaning
BL:NAME	Extract the name of blocks
BL:NUMBER	Count the number of occurrences of each block
PRODUCT, STOCKNO	Extract the values of attributes with PRODUCT and STOCKNO tags
C008000	Format as character (C), eight spaces wide
N003000	Format as number (N), three spaces wide (003) and with zero decimal places (000)

STEP 2: EXTRACT ATTRIBUTE DATA (File|Import/Export|Attributes Out)

1. If necessary, launch AutoCAD LT and load the ELECTRIC drawing.

2. Start the AttExt command by selecting **File|Import/Export| Attributes Out** from the menu bar. AutoCAD displays the Attribute Extraction dialog box.

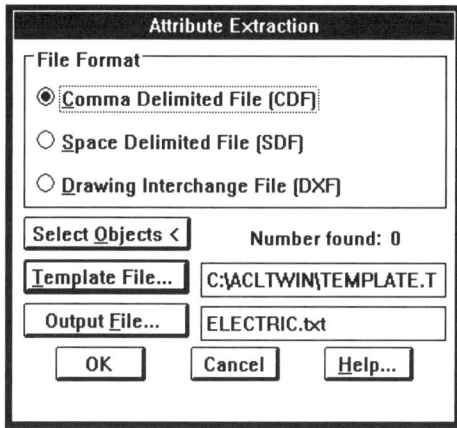

3. Under **File Format**, you have the choice of three output formats:
   - CDF (command-delimited format) separates values by commas and is best suited for importing attribute data in spreadsheets and word processors.
   - SDF (space-delimited format) separates values by spaces and is best suited for importing data into database programs.
   - DXF (drawing interchange format) exports data in AutoCAD's own DXF format and is best suited for programmers.

Make sure that the CDF radio button is selected.

4. Click on the **Select Objects** button. AutoCAD prompts you, as follows:
   Command: _ddattext
   Select objects: **all**
   124 found Select objects: **[Enter]**

When you specify All, AutoCAD selects all suitable objects in the entire drawing, which is faster than using Window or Crossing mode.

5. Click on the **Template File** button. When the Template File dialog box appears, select **TEMPLATE.TXT**, the attribute extract template file you created earlier, which is probably in your WINDOWS directory.

Hour 7

6. Click on the **OK** button. AutoCAD searches through the drawing, counting each instance of every component. After a second or two, the results are deposited in the ELECTRIC.TXT file. You can examine it with Notepad, as shown in the figure below:

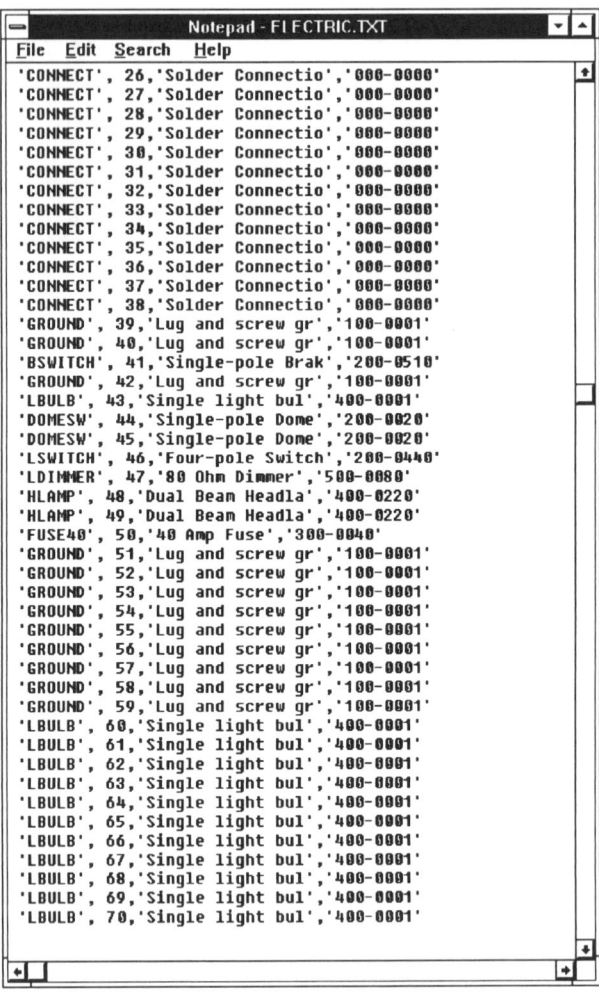

For each block you placed in the ELECTRIC drawing, AutoCAD listed the block's name, the number of its occurrences, followed by the product name and stock number. You've now created a rudimentary bill of material which can be printed out on your printer or imported to a spreadsheet.

Bills of Material

STEP 3: IMPORTING THE BOM INTO EXCEL

The steps shown here for importing the extracted attribute data (bill of material) into a spreadsheet are for Microsoft Excel. Lotus 1-2-3 and Borland Quattro have analogous steps. You can also import the BOM into a database, which may be more useful.

1. In the Windows Program Manager, launch Excel 4.0 by double-clicking on its icon. (Use the same general approach if you are using Excel 5.0.)
2. Start a new worksheet by selecting **File|Open** to display the Open dialog box.
3. Select **Text Files (*.prn; *.txt; *.csv)**, pick **ELECTRIC.TXT**, and click **OK**. When Excel displays the new dialog box, click on the **Comma** radio button and make sure that **Windows (ANSI)** is selected. Click on the **OK** button.

    ### NOTE
    If you are using Excel 5.0, work with the Text Import Wizard. Set Delimiters to Comma and click the Finish button. Move to step 6.

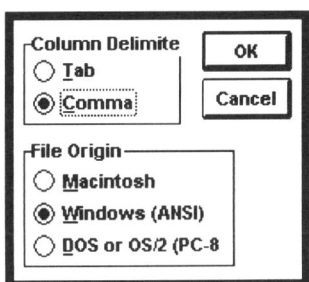

4. Move to the subdirectory where ELECTRIC.TXT is located and change the File Name from *.XL* to ***.TXT**.
5. Select **ELECTRIC.TXT** and click on the **OK** button.
6. Excel loads the ELECTRIC.TXT file, displaying each field in its own column. Use the **Format|Column Width|Best Fit** command to adjust the column widths.

Hour 7

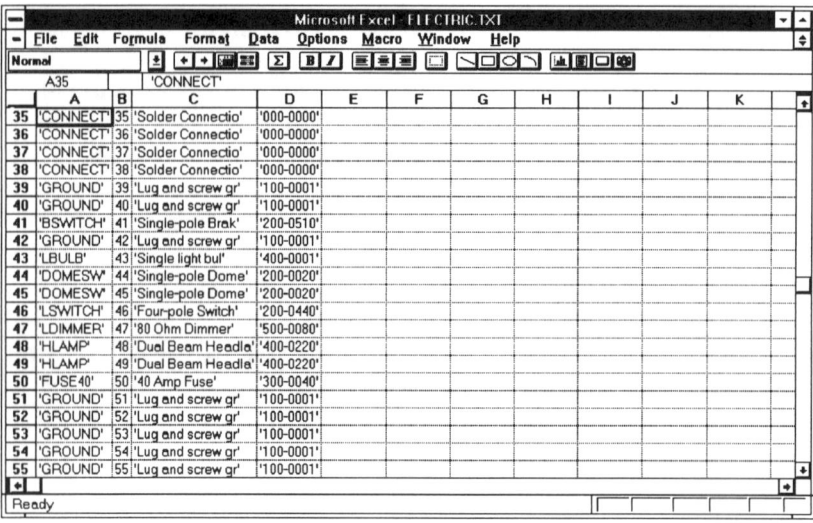

7. Add price and extension fields, a totals row, and format the text for an attractive output. The formula to count the number of items in column B is:

=count(B3:B72)

And the formula to add up the total cost in column E is:

=sum(E3:E72)

Remember to save the worksheet as an XLS file.

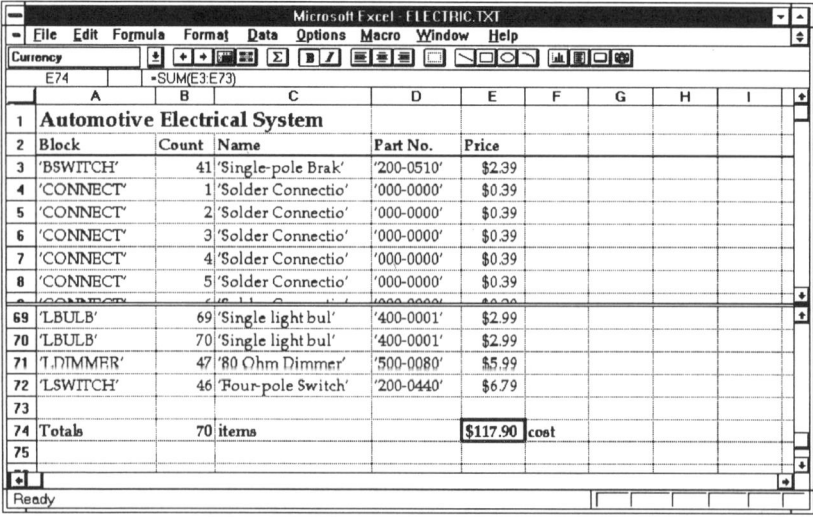

Bills of Material

While AutoCAD quickly exports bill of material information, it has no method for bringing the data back into the drawing as a table.

SUMMARY

In this hour, you learned to create "bill of material" information with the AttExt command. You also learned how to bring the attribute data into a spreadsheet.

In the next chapter, you learn how to do simple programming of AutoCAD to reduce keystrokes.

Hour 8
PROGRAMMING AUTOCAD MACROS

INTRODUCTION

In the previous hour, you learned how to increase your CAD efficiency by creating components and attributes. These let AutoCAD insert and count commonly used symbols much faster than you could do it.

In this chapter, you learn how to decrease your keystroke count even further by programming AutoCAD's toolbar and toolbox with macros.

CUSTOMIZING THE TOOLBAR

Many software programs have a macro programming language, and AutoCAD LT is no exception. A "macro" is a series of keystrokes. If you do a common series of commands over and over again, then you may want to turn them into a macro.

First, let's look at AutoCAD's toolbar.

1. Start AutoCAD with a new drawing named "MACROS."
2. Look at the toolbar, located directly below the menu bar. As mentioned in Hour 1, the number of iconic buttons you see on the toolbar depends on the size of the AutoCAD window and other factors. At the very most, you see a total of 31 buttons on a high-resolution screen.

The five leftmost buttons (color, Layer, down-arrow, O, S, and P) are fixed and cannot be changed. The rightmost buttons (you will see up to 26 depending on the window size) can be modified by you to run macros. Autodesk has preprogrammed 17 of the 26 buttons.

You can change the size of the buttons on the toolbar. The size of the buttons is changed with the SetEnv command and the ToolBarSize environment variable. The size is measured in pixels. The smallest size allowed by AutoCAD is six pixels.

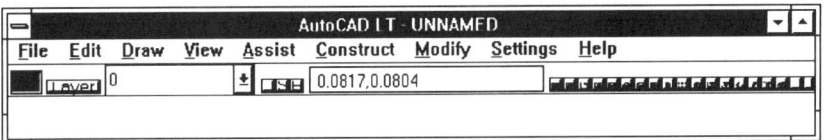

As you can see from the figures, smaller buttons let you see more buttons on the toolbar but are hard to read. The largest size for the toolbar buttons is 30 pixels.

As the figure shows, larger buttons are easier to read but allow fewer buttons on the toolbar.

3. You change the size of the toolbar buttons as follows:

   Command: **setenv**
   Variable name: **toolbarsize**
   Value <16>: **[enter a number between 6 and 30]**

For the new button size to come into effect, you must exit AutoCAD LT and start it again.

4. You can also change the size and font of the text displayed on the toolbar and the command prompt area. If you have difficulty reading the AutoCAD screen, you will find it useful to change to a larger font. Select **File|Preferences|Fonts** from the menu bar. AutoCAD displays the Fonts dialog box.

123

Hour 8

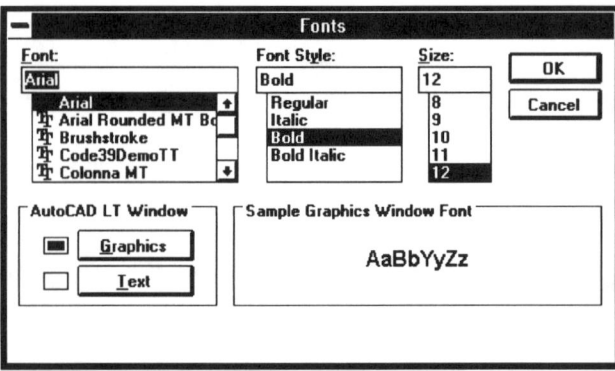

5. Scroll through the list of font names. Arial is a font included with every Windows package and is particularly easy to read. Click on its name.
6. Select the **Bold** attribute to make the font slightly darker.
7. Select a font size of **12** (the largest size AutoCAD LT permits).
8. Click on the two **OK** buttons to clear the dialog boxes. Unlike the toolbar size, the font change comes into effect immediately. The figure below shows the 12-point Arial Bold font with 24-pixel toolbar icons.

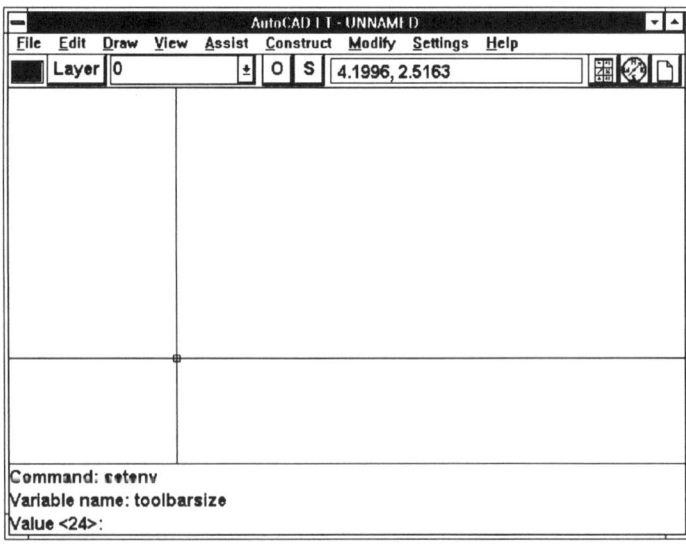

PREPROGRAMMED MACROS

To become familiar with toolbar macros, let's first look at how Autodesk preprogrammed these buttons.

1. Move the cursor to the toolbar and position the cursor over the first programmable icon button (the toolbox button, which looks like a dirty window).
2. Click your mouse's rightmost button. AutoCAD displays the Toolbar Button 1 Customization dialog box.

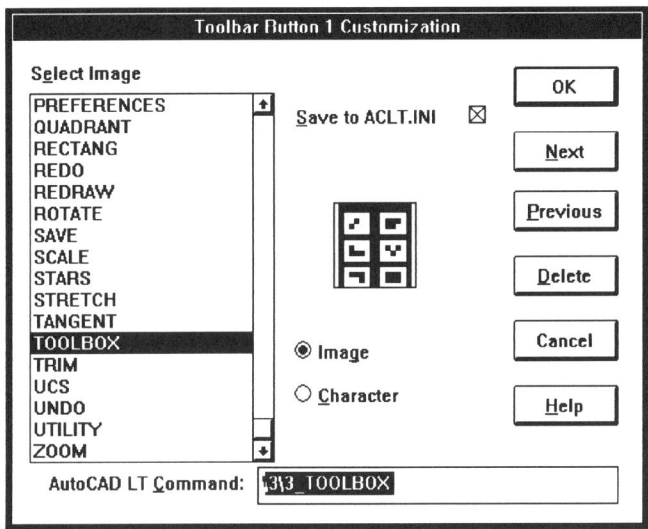

The dialog box lets you do three things: (1) define the macro (text box at the bottom); (2) assign a predefined image or character to the button (the list at the right); and (3) move along to the next button (buttons at the left).

3. Button 1 is defined by this simple macro:

   \3\3_TOOLBOX

The macro cancels any command in progress, then executes the Toolbox command. Let's see what each part of this macro does:

- The \3 means "cancel." It cancels any existing command and is the equivalent of pressing Ctrl+C. If no command is in progress, AutoCAD ignores the \3. Two \3 in a row cancels commands that have several layers of options, such as the PEdit and Dim commands.
- The underscore (_) prefix ensures that any language of AutoCAD can execute the command.
- TOOLBOX is the AutoCAD command that toggles the display of the toolbox.
- A space after TOOLBOX (it's hard to see but it's there!) is the equivalent of pressing the Enter key. Since it's hard to see the space, AutoCAD automatically adds it for you.

A single click on button 1 executes the equivalent of ten keystrokes, a real time saver!

4. Click on the **Next** button. AutoCAD displays information about the next (to the right) icon button. As you click repeatedly on the Next button, you see the macros defined by each button. The buttons visible on a VGA screen have these macros:

\3\3_TOOLBOX
_DSVIEWER
\3\3_NEW
\3\3_OPEN
\3\3_SAVE
\3\3_PLOT

Each follows the format of the first macro: \3\3 cancels a command in progress; _ ensures international compatibility; the command name, followed by a single space character.

The exception is the _DSVIEWER command. Since it has no \3\3 prefix, the command can be activated during another command without cancelling it.

5. If AutoCAD has a larger window, you also see additional buttons with these macros:

'_ZOOM
'_PAN
'_REDRAW
'_DDRMODES
@
.X

.Y
_CLOSE
_U
_REDO
\3\3

The first four macros are prefixed by an apostrophe ('). Recall that this indicates a transparent command, which can run during another command.

All of the special characters recognized by AutoCAD in toolbar macros are shown in the table below:

Character	Meaning
space	Enter
\2	Toggle snap mode on and off
\3	Cancel current command
\4	Toggle coordinate display modes
\5	Toggle isometric drawing planes
\7	Toggle visibility of grid
\n	New line (acts like a carriage return)
\\	The \ character
;	Suppress the addition of the space suffix

CHANGING A MACRO

Now that you have seen what a macro looks like (albeit very a simple macro), try changing the macro assigned to button #4. Change the button's action from the Open command to the DdInsert command, which displays the Insert dialog box.

1. Click the right mouse button on icon button #4. AutoCAD displays the Toolbar Button 4 Customization dialog box.
2. Change the AutoCAD LT Command: text from \3\3_OPEN to:

   '_ddinsert

This macro executes DdInsert as a transparent command. It doesn't matter whether the words are uppercase or lowercase.

3. In the Select Image box, click on **DDINSERT** to display an icon (you cannot create a custom icon for AutoCAD LT).

Hour 8

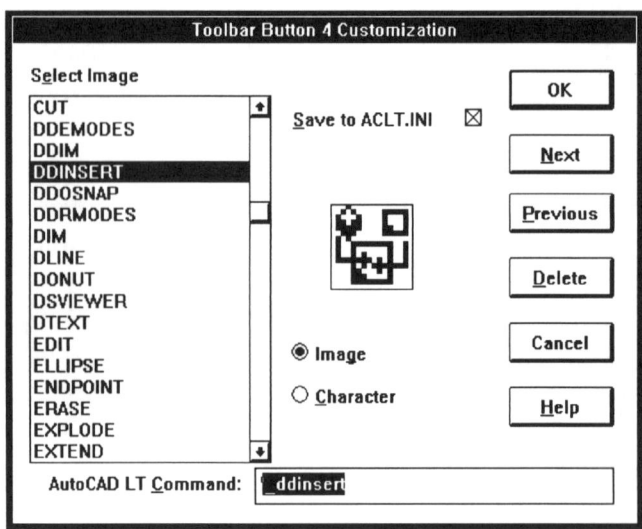

4. If you don't like the icon, you have two choices:
   - Select any other icon from the list of 81 provided by Autodesk.
   - Click on the **Character** radio button. The list of icon names changes to the alphabet. Select a meaningful character, such as D or I.

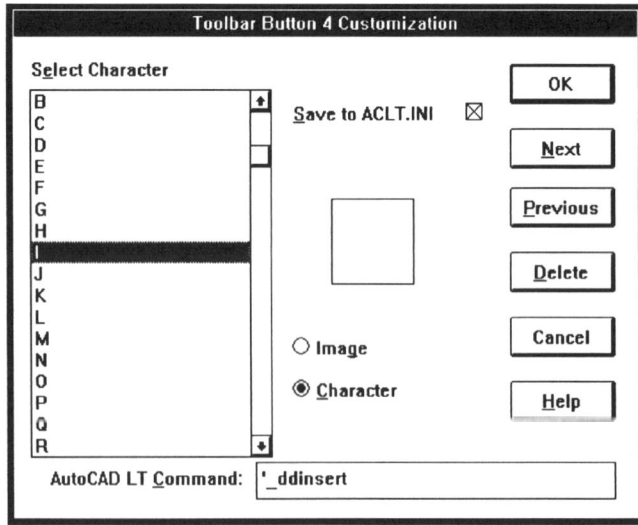

5. Make sure the check box next to **Save to ACLT.INI** is turned on. Click on the **OK** button to finish the macro redefinition.
6. Congratulations! You've written your first macro! By clicking on button #4 you want AutoCAD to execute the DdInsert command. Try using the newly defined button. Click on button #4 and AutoCAD displays the Insert dialog box. Click on the **Cancel** button to remove it.

MULTI-COMMAND MACROS

By programming the button with the DdInsert command as a macro, you cut your menu picks in half! However, you can go much further by stringing several commands together. AutoCAD LT lets you define macros of up to 254 characters in length (the 255th character needs to reserved for the space character). Let's see how that works by redefining button #4 with three commands.

A useful command sequence is to save the drawing, zoom all, then plot the drawing. With the fragile state of Windows printer drivers, it is important to save your work before printing; zooming out lets you see the entire drawing.

1. The commands you would type in are:
   Command: **qsave**
   Command: **zoom a**
   Command: **plot**

That's 18 keystrokes. If you pick commands from the menu bar, you would select:

File|Save
View|Zoom|All
File|Plot

Add them up: that's seven menu picks to store your drawing and editing changes to the safety of a disk file.

2. To combine the 18 keystrokes (or seven menu picks) into a single macro, write down the keys you press in order, as follows:
   qsave
   zoom a
   plot

Hour 8

The keystroke syntax is important since AutoCAD does not tolerate incorrect keystrokes. Pressing the wrong key stalls the command sequence. In the same way, supplying the wrong character in the macro stalls the command.

3. In an AutoCAD macro, commands must be separated by spaces and placed on a single line. Also, it is useful to prefix the macro with the cancel sequence (\3\3) and internationalize the commands with the underscore (_). Thus, our macro looks like this:

   \3\3_qsave _zoom a _plot

Remember to end the macro with no space.

4. Now that you have defined the macro that saves and plots the drawing, let's define a new toolbox button. If the toolbox is not visible on the screen, type in the Toolbox command, as follows:

   Command: **toolbox**

5. Right-click on any icon.

6. When the Toolbox Customization dialog box appears, click on the **Insert** button.

7. The dialog box disappears and the icon is duplicated on the toolbox. Right-click on the duplicate button and the Toolbox Customization dialog box appears again.

8. Next to AutoCAD LT Command, type the macro:

   \3\3_qsave _zoom a _plot

9. Select a suitable icon from the Image Name list, such as UTILITY.

Programming AutoCAD Macros

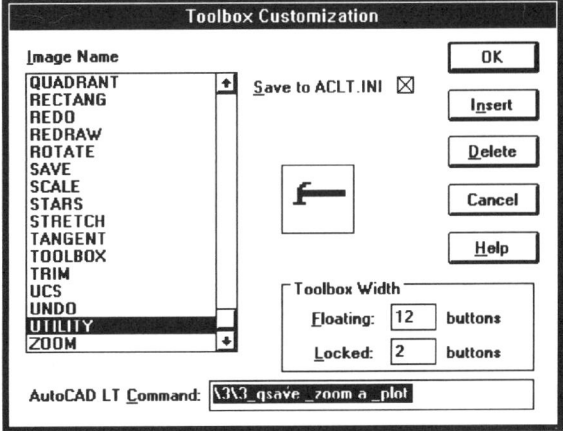

10. Make sure the check box next to Save to ACLT.INI is on. Click on the **OK** button to save the changes and dismiss the dialog box.

11. The new hammer icon appears on the toolbox. Click on it to save the drawing, zoom out full, and bring up the Plot Control dialog box. (Click on the **Cancel** button if you don't want to plot at this time.)

SUMMARY

The drawback to AutoCAD LT's macros is that they cannot pause for user input. This limits their usefulness. Still, in this hour you learned how to assign many keystrokes to a single toolbar or toolbox button to work more efficiently.

AutoCAD LT also includes menu macro and Diesel programming commands that are more powerful than macro keystrokes. If programming interests you, refer to Chapter 15 of the User's Guide manual that accompanies the AutoCAD LT for Windows package.

Appendix A
SETTING UP AUTOCAD LT FOR WINDOWS

INTRODUCTION

You must set up the AutoCAD LT software package before you can use it for computer-aided drafting. This appendix describes the computer hardware need to run AutoCAD LT and shows you how to install the AutoCAD LT software package.

COMPUTER HARDWARE REQUIREMENTS

The AutoCAD LT diskette #1 contains a setup program that copies the files from the distribution diskettes onto your computer's hard disk. Before installing AutoCAD, first check that your computer has the hardware required to run Windows and AutoCAD.

Operating System AutoCAD LT for Windows works only with the Microsoft Windows 3.1 operating system running in enhanced mode. AutoCAD LT does not work until Windows is first installed and running on your computer.

CPU To run AutoCAD LT for Windows, your computer must be an IBM-compatible that uses an Intel 80386-compatible CPU, such as 80386, 80486SX, 80486DX, or Pentium. An 80387-compatible math chip is required in 386-based and 486SX-based computers.

Memory If your computer is able to run Windows 3.1 in enhanced mode, then it probably has enough memory to run AutoCAD LT. However, AutoCAD is a program that uses a lot of memory. Thus,

Setting Up AutoCAD LT for Windows

while AutoCAD LT will load on a computer with 4MB RAM memory, it will run slowly. You will have better AutoCAD (and Windows) performance when your computer has at least 8MB RAM memory.

Disk Drives The computer must have an IBM-compatible 3-1/2" 1.44MB floppy drive to read the AutoCAD diskettes. If your computer has only a 5-1/4" 1.2MB floppy drive, the AutoCAD LT package includes a coupon for obtaining the appropriate diskettes.

To store the AutoCAD program, your computer's hard drive needs at least 10MB of space free on the hard disk, plus additional space for storing the drawings you will be creating.

Tip: You can reclaim about 4MB of disk space by not loading the symbol library and by deleting the LT Tutor (erase the tbk*.*, *.tbk and tutorial.hlp files).

Autodesk (and Microsoft) recommend that Windows run with a permanent swap file at least as large as your computer's RAM memory.

Tip: To set up a swap file, in the Windows Program Manager double-click on the Control Panel icon, then double-click on the 386 Enhanced icon. When the 386 Enhanced dialog box appears, click on the Virtual Memory button. When the Virtual Memory dialog box appears, click on the Change button. Change the Type to permanent and accept the size suggested by Windows.

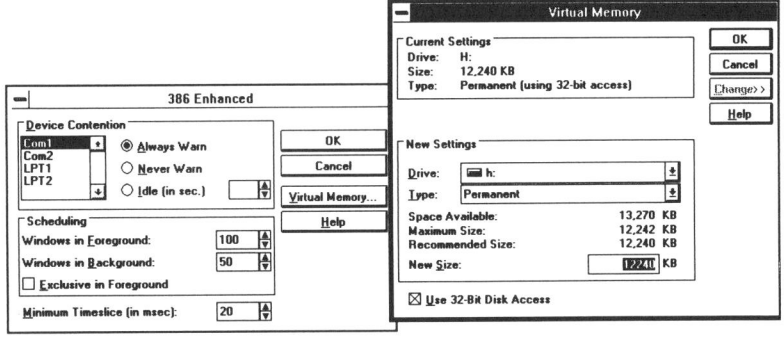

Peripherals AutoCAD LT works with any peripheral that works with Windows. "Peripherals" include the graphics board, display monitor, mouse, and printer. While Windows and LT works with VGA resolution (640x480), a higher resolution is recommend—at least SuperVGA (800x600). It doesn't matter whether the monitor displays monochrome or color.

133

Appendix A

While most CAD packages work with a digitizing tablet and pen plotter, AutoCAD LT does not support tablets and plotters except through an appropriate Windows device driver. Contact the digitizer and plotter vendor for a Window driver.

Tip: Most pen plotters are compatible with Hewlett-Packard plotters. Try configuring Windows with any HP Plotter driver by double-clicking on the Printers icon in the Control Panel. When the Printers dialog box appears, first click on the Add>> button to select the plotter, then click on the Setup button to set up the plotter's parameters.

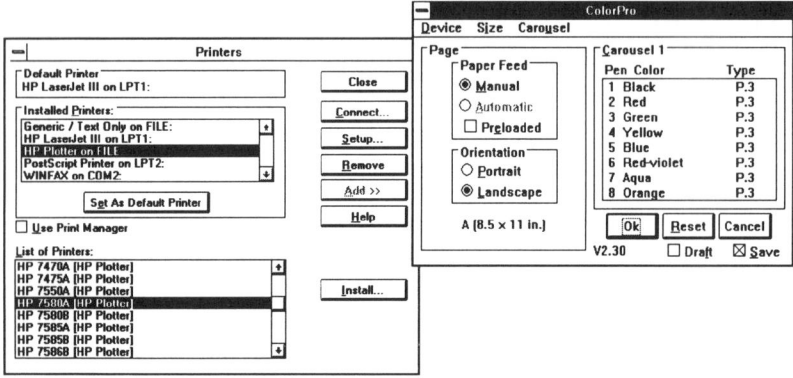

INSTALLING AUTOCAD LT FOR WINDOWS

AutoCAD LT comes with a setup program that copies the AutoCAD diskettes onto the computer's hard drive.

1. Before you begin the Setup program, use the Windows File Manager to check that your computer's hard disk has at least 10MB of free space. If your computer has more than one hard drive, set up AutoCAD on the drive with the most free disk space. Don't install AutoCAD at all unless one hard drive has at least 8MB free disk space.

2. The software license permits you to make a backup copy of the diskettes onto another set of diskettes. A backup set is useful if one of the original diskettes is lost or damaged (by virus, heat, or theft). From DOS, use the **Diskcopy** command; from Windows, use the File Manager's **Disk|Copy Disk** command. (The vertical

bar, |, is shorthand to select the Disk item from the menu bar. When the menu appears, select Copy Disk.)

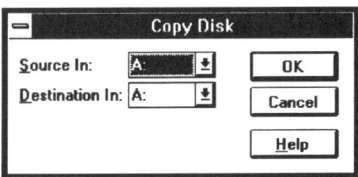

3. If you plan to install the symbols library, make sure your computer is running a disk cache and that the floppy drive is read-cached. Without the cache, the more than 300 symbol files take a long time to copy; with the cache, the setup time is reduced from a half-hour down to about five minutes.
4. Run the Setup program by inserting AutoCAD LT Disk 1 into the floppy drive and close the door.
5. In the Windows Program Manager, select **File|Run** from the menu bar.
6. When the Run dialog box appears, type:
   Command line: **a:\setup**

   and click on the **OK** button. The Setup program loads and displays a dialog box congratulating you on your purchase.

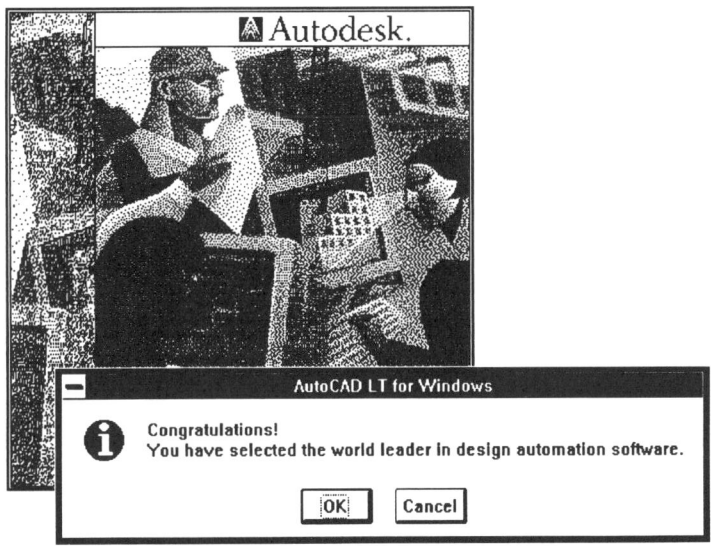

Appendix A

7. The Setup program suggests placing the software in c:\acltwin. That means drive C: and subdirectory \acltwin. If your computer has one hard drive, then the only answer is C:. If your computer has more than one hard drive, you have a choice; change the drive name to one with the most free space.

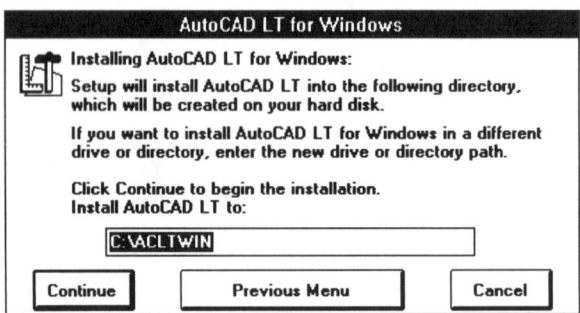

The Setup program also needs to know in which subdirectory to install AutoCAD. Mostly likely, you use the name supplied as the default, acltwin. Since the directory probably doesn't exist, the Setup program creates it for you.

8. The Setup program asks you to type your name and company name. This information is added to AutoCAD LT, personalizing the program for you. After you enter the information, Install asks you for confirmation since the data is permanently written to the AutoCAD file.

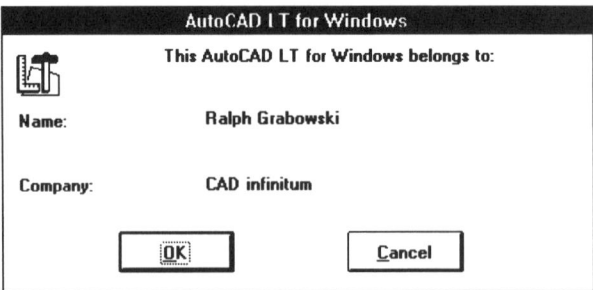

9. Now it's decision time. The Setup program can install all of AutoCAD LT's files or just some of them. If you are short on disk space, then you may not want to install the symbol library at this time (you can run Setup again later to add the symbols).

136

Setting Up AutoCAD LT for Windows

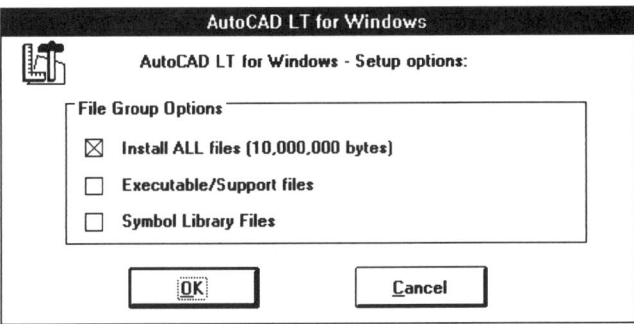

10. The Setup program begins copying files from the AutoCAD diskettes to the hard disk.

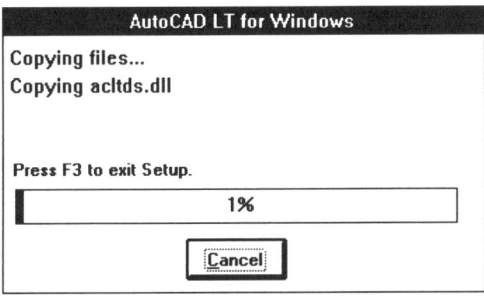

When the Setup program prompts you, remove the diskette and insert the next diskette.

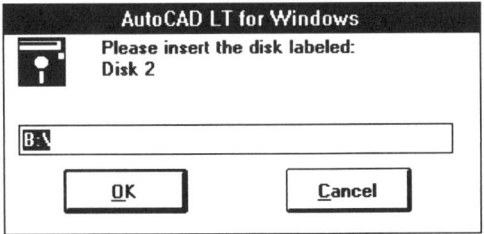

11. After all AutoCAD diskettes are copied onto the hard drive, the Setup program asks you for the program group name for the Windows Program Manager. Accept the default and Setup creates a new program group; or, type the name of an existing program group.

Appendix A

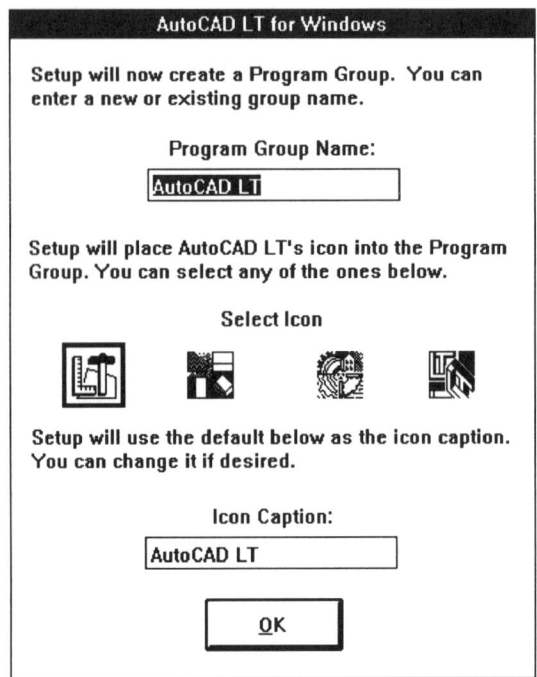

Setup gives you a choice of four icons for AutoCAD LT. Pick the one that appeals to you.

12. If you have another version of AutoCAD already installed (such as AutoCAD Release 12 for Windows), the Setup program asks if you want to change the association for DWG files. "Association" means that Windows will automatically launch AutoCAD LT (or Release 12) when you double-click on a DWG (drawing) type of file. Unfortunately, Windows can only associate one program with a file type; thus, you must decide if the DWG file automatically loads AutoCAD Release 12 or AutoCAD LT. (You can still use either program to load the DWG file.)

Setting Up AutoCAD LT for Windows

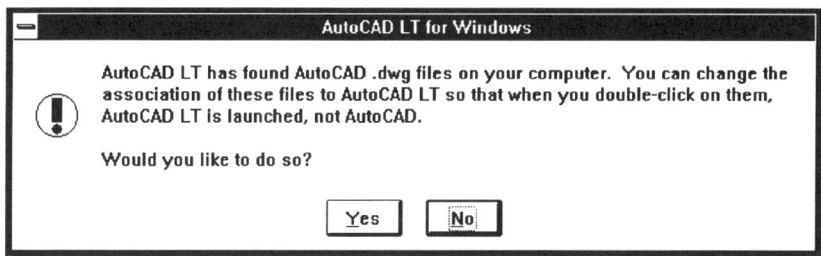

13. The Install program is now finished. Remove the last AutoCAD diskette from the floppy drive and store all the diskettes in a safe place (like your safety deposit box).

14. Start AutoCAD LT by double-clicking on the icon created by the Setup program.

If you are familiar with other versions of AutoCAD, relax: you don't need to do anything to configure AutoCAD LT. AutoCAD is now ready to use.

You can start with the lessons in Hour 1, Setting Up the Drawing, where you learn how to set up AutoCAD LT for your first drawing.

Appendix B
INSTALLING AND USING THE BONUS DISK

INTRODUCTION

This book includes a bonus diskette. The diskette contains a copy of the three work drawings, yard.dwg, symbols.dwg, and electric.dwg.

The diskette contains additional files:

- DWG drawing files that show what the drawing looks like at the end of each hour. If you make mistakes during one hour, you can start with a clean drawing the next hour.
- Individual DWG drawing files of the electrical symbols (blocks and attributes) created in Hour 6.
- The TXT and XLS files created in Hour 7 for attribute extraction.

This appendix describes the files on the bonus disk and tells you how to copy the files from the bonus disk to your computer.

DWG DRAWING FILES

The drawings are given their chapter names:

Filename	Contents
hour1.dwg	Yard drawing at the end of Hour 1
hour2.dwg	Yard drawing at the end of Hour 2
hour3.dwg	Yard drawing at the end of Hour 3
hour4.dwg	Yard drawing at the end of Hour 4

Filename	Contents (Continued)
hour5.dwg	Yard drawing at the end of Hour 5
yard.dwg	Completed yard drawing
hour6.dwg	Electric drawing at end of Hour 6
symbols.dwg	Completed symbols drawing
hour7.dwg	Electric drawing at end of Hour 7
electric.dwg	Completed electric drawing

1. Copy the drawings from the bonus diskette to your computer's hard disk. If the bonus diskette is in the A: floppy drive, and AutoCAD LT resides on the C: hard drive, then type the following at the DOS prompt:

    C:\> **copy a:*.* c:\acltwin**

    Or,

    Use the Windows File Manager to copy the file from the floppy drive to the hard drive.

2. To load one of the bonus drawings into AutoCAD LT, select **File|Open** from the menu bar. When the dialog box appears, double-click on a filename from the list of drawing names listed. The drawing is displayed on the graphics screen.

DWG BLOCK AND TXT ATTRIBUTE FILES

The diskette also contains the block and attribute files created in Hour 6. These files are stored in the diskette's Symbols subdirectory:

Filename	Contents
bswitch.dwg	Brake switch symbol
connect.dwg	Connection symbol
domesw.dwg	Dome switch symbol
fuse40.dwg	Fuse symbol
ground.dwg	Ground symbol
hlamp.dwg	Headlamp symbol
lbulb.dwg	Light bulb symbol
ldimmer.dwg	Light dimmer symbol
lswitch.dwg	Light switch symbol
template.txt	Attribute extraction template file
electric.txt	Extracted attributes
electric.xls	Excel worksheet with attributes

Copy the block and attributes files from the bonus diskette to your computer's hard disk. If the bonus diskette is in the A: floppy drive, and AutoCAD LT resides on the C: hard drive, then type the following at the DOS prompt:

C:\> **copy a:\symbols*.* c:\acltwin\symbols**

Or,

Use the Windows File Manager to copy the file from the floppy drive to the hard drive.

Index

A Fast Way to Place Text, 84
Absolute coordinates, 25
Adding a Fence, 71
Adding Details to the Landscape Plan, 40
Adding Many More Trees, 54
Adding Notes and Dimensions, 76
Adding the Street and Driveway, 33
Aerial View, 54-55
Align, text, 80
Aligned and Radial Dimensions, 91
Angles and bearings in a drawing, 17
Apostrophe, transparent command, 48
Architectural units (feet and inches), 16
Area command, 70
Array, 50
Array command, 52
Assist|Area, 70
Assist|Distance, 74
Assist|Object Snap, 71
Assist|XYZ Filters, 71
Attribute Extract Template File, 116
Attribute fields, 99
Attributes, 94
AutoCAD LT Symbols, 97
AutoCAD Window, 3
Automatic Save, 22

Baseline dimensions, 90
Basic Procedures, Help, 12
Bills of Material, 115
Block, 53
Block Definition dialog box, 53
Blocks, storing on disk, 105
Bonus Disk, 141
Border, 65
Bringing Back the Yard Drawing, 24
Buttons, displayed, 7-9

Cancel command, 11

Change command, 82
Change Points, 66
Change property, 64
Changing a Macro, 127
Changing Existing Text, 81
Changing Layers, 26
Changing Line Lengths, 65
Changing the Landscape, 62
Changing the Look of Lines, 62
Changing the Look of the Pond, 66
Changing the Text Font, 78
ChProp command, 64
Circle, 50
Clear All button, 20
Color button, 5
Combining the Symbol and Attribute into a Block, 103
Command Area, 10
Commands, ways to invoke, 27
Computer Hardware Requirements, 132
Construct|Array, 50, 52
Construct|Define Attribute, 100
Construct|Fillet, 33-34
Construct|Make Block, 103
Construct|Mirror, 33-35
Construct|Offset, 60
Context-Sensitive Help, 12-13
Coordinate Display, 7
Coordinate notation, 25
Copyright notice, 2
CPU, 132
Create a New Drawing, 15
Creating a Symbol, 50
Creating New Layers, 19
Creating Symbols and Attributes, 94
Creating the Attribute Fields, 99
Creating the Hatch Boundary, 46
Creating the Other Blocks, 108
Crosshair Cursor, 3
Ctrl+C, 11

Cursor, 3
Customizing the Toolbar, 122

Decimal units, 16
Define Attribute, 100
Degrees, fractional, 17
Dimension text, 87
Dimensioning the Yard (DimScale), 86
Dimensions, aligned, 91
Dimensions, radial, 91
Dimscale command, 87
Disk Drives, 133
Disk, Bonus, 140
Dist command, 74
Distance, 74
Dividing the Lot, 40
Donut command, 98
Draw|Arc|Start, Center, End command, 110
Draw|Circle, 50
Draw|Donut, 98
Draw|Ellipse, 59
Draw|Insert Block, 54, 56
Draw|Linear Dimensions, 87
Draw|Linear Dimensions|Vertical, 89
Draw|Radial Dimensions|Radius, 92
Draw|Text, 76, 84
Drawing Aids, 17, 96
Drawing area, 3
Drawing the Electrical Schematic, 111
Drawing the First Symbol, 98
Drawing the House Outline (Draw|Polyline, Assist|Object Snap), 28
Drawing the Lot Boundary (Draw|Line), 25
Drawing the Pond, 59
Drawing the Yard Outline, 24
Dsviewer command, 54
Dtext command, 83

Edit Polyline, 42
Edit Text, 82

Ellipse command, 59
ENDpoint object snap, 112
Enter key, 11
Exit Help, 14
Extract Attribute Data, 116

F2 (AutoCAD LT Text), 11-12
Feet and fractional inches, 16
File Format, 117
File Locking, 23
File|Import/Export|Attributes Out, 116
File|Import/Export|Block Out, 105
File|Import/Export|Wmf In, 106
File|Preferences, 22
File|Print/Plot, 36-38
File|Yard, 24
Fillet command, 33-34
Flipscreen key (F2), 12
Floating toolbox, 3
Font, text, 78
Full menu, 4

Geometric object snaps, 29
Graphics Screen, 12
Grid, 17-18
Grips (blue squares), 44

Hatch, 49-50
Hatching the Lawn (Draw|Hatch), 49
Height of text, 77
Help Window, 12
Horizontal and Continuous Dimensions, 87

Icons, 8
Import WMF, 107
Importing the BOM Into Excel, 119
Insert Block, 56, 104
Installing and Using the Bonus Disk, 140
Installing AutoCAD LT for Windows, 134

Justification, text, 80

Layer button, 6

Index

Layer command options, 27
Layer control, 20
Layer Control dialog box, 7
Layer names, 19, 21
Layers, 19
Layers, changing, 26
Limits, 18
Line command, 10
Linear Dimensions, 87
Linetype command, 63
List Block Names, 58
Loading Blocks from Disk, 106

Macros, 122
Make Block, 53
Making a Symbol (Contruct|Make Block), 53
Measurement expression, 16
Measurement notation, 18
Measuring the Area of the Lawn, 70
Memory, 132
Menu bar, 4
Menu symbols, 5
Meters and centimeters, 16
Mirror command, 34-35
Modes, 17
Modify|Change Point, 66, 82
Modify|Edit Polyline, 42
Modify|Edit Text, 82
Modify|Move, 31-32
Modify|Stretch, 66
Move command, 31-32, 69
Moving the House Into Position, 31
Multi-Command Macros, 129

Name the Drawing, 15
New file, 15
Non-Modal Editing, 43

Object snap modes, 40
Object snaps, geometric, 29
Obliquing angle, text, 79
Offset command, 60
Operating System, 132
Ortho Mode, 7

Pan, 59

Paper Space, 7
Pedit command, 42-43
Peripherals, 133
Pline command, 29-30, 40, 71
Point filters, 73
Polyline, 28, 40, 71
Precision list box, Units, 16
Preferences dialog box, 22
Preparing for Drawing the Symbol, 95
Preparing for Drawing the Yard, 15
Preprogrammed Macros, 125
Print/Plot, 36
Printing the drawing, 36
Programming AutoCAD Macros, 122
Prompt, attribute, 100
Putting the Drawing on Paper, 36

QText command, 85-86
Quick Text, 85

Radio button, 16
Radius, Dimensions, 92
Redraw command, 32
Reducing Text Display Time, 85
Regen command, 51
Relative coordinates, 25
Reshaping a polyline, 45
Resolution, 8
Rotation angle, text, 77
Rubber band line, 10

Save view, 80
Saving for security, 22
Saving the Drawing, 21
Scale factor, text, 77
Schematic sketch, 95
Search dialog box, Help, 14
Searching, Help, 14
Select color, 6
Select Objects button, block, 103
Selecting the Components, 96
Set Color button, 20
Setting the drawing Limits (paper size), 18

145

Setting the Units, 16
Setting Up AutoCAD LT for Windows, 132
Setting Up The Drawing, 1
Settings menu, 4
Settings, Units Style, 16
Settings|Linetype Style|Load, 63
Settings|Text Style, 78
Setup program, 2
Shift+right mouse button, object snap modes, 40
Short menu, 4
SHX font format, 78
Smoothing the Polyline, 42
Snap and Grid, 17-18
Snap Mode, 7
Starting AutoCAD LT, 2
Status line, 22
Storing Blocks on Disk, 105
Stretch, 45
Stretch command, 66
SVGA resolution, 8
Symbols, 94
Symbols, AutoCAD LT, 97

Tag, attribute, 100
TEMPLATE.TXT, 117
Text command, 76

Text scale factor, 77
Text Style, 78
Text Window, 11
Title bar, 4
Toolbar, 3, 5
Toolbar Buttons, 7
Toolbox, 9
Transparent command, 48

Undo, 33
Units Style, 16
Units, setting, 16

Value, attribute, 100
Vertical and Baseline Dimensions, 89
VGA resolution, 8
View, Aerial, 55
View|Redraw, 31-32
View|Save, 80
View|Zoom Window, 43

Width, text, 79
WMF files, 97

x-, y-coordinates, 7

Zoom All command, 19
Zoom Window, 43